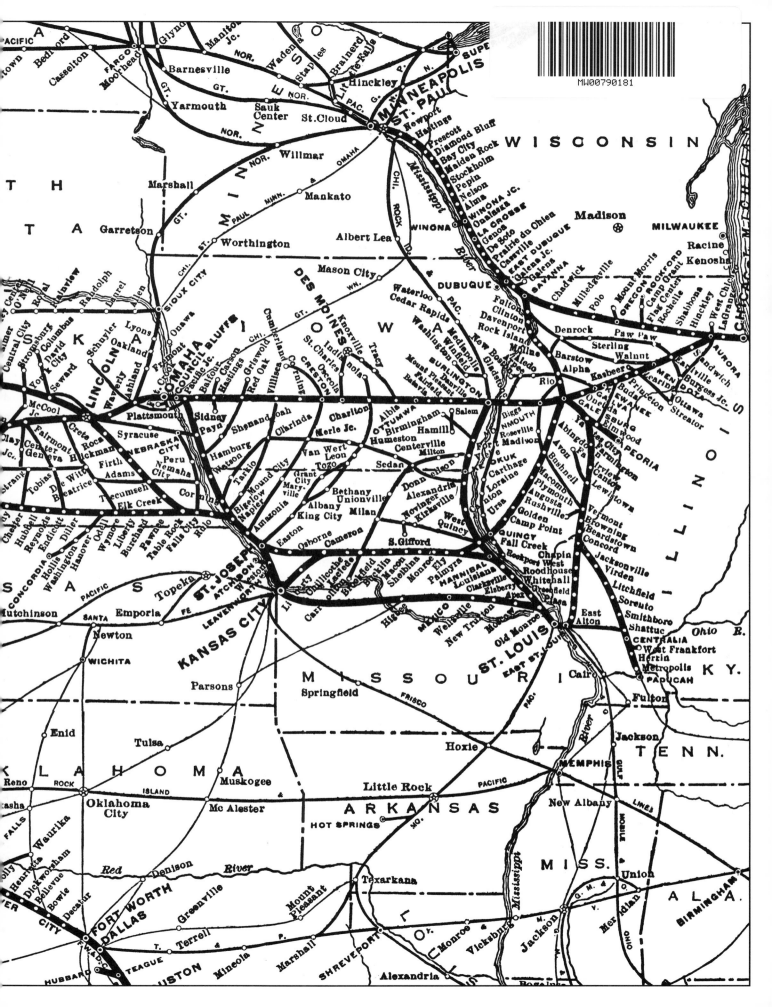

Burlington Route

The Early Zephyrs

Geoffrey H. Doughty

© Copyright 2002 TLC Publishing, Inc
1387 Winding Creek Lane
Lynchburg, Virginia 24503-3776

International Standard Book Number   1-883089-66-2
Library of Congress Catalog Card Number 2001093711

Art Direction, Editing, and Production by
Kevin J. Holland
type&DESIGN
Burlington, Ontario

Produced on the MacOS™

Printed by
Walsworth Publishing Company
Marceline, Missouri 64658

Front cover painting ©Andrew Harmantas
Bystanders witness the dawn of a new era in railroad passenger service as the stainless steel *Burlington Zephyr* makes its triumphant non-stop run from Denver to Chicago on May 26, 1934.

Frontispiece and title page images, Kevin J. Holland Collection

Other books by Geoffrey H. Doughty from TLC Publishing, Inc.—

New York Central and the Trains of the Future
New York Central Lightweight Passenger Cars, Trains and Travel
New York Central's Great Steel Fleet, 1948–1967
New York Central's Stations and Terminals
The New Haven Railroad in the Streamline Era
The New Haven Railroad's Streamline Passenger Fleet, 1934–1953
Canadian Treasures—Two Trains Across Canada

In memory of Richard C. Overton

Historian, Teacher

ACKNOWLEDGMENTS

First and foremost, this book would not have been written if it were not for Richard C. Overton, a.k.a Uncle Dick, a close family friend for three generations. It was he who introduced me to the Burlington when I was a little boy and I was overjoyed then to have an uncle who could talk trains with me. As I grew up, he was a constant pen pal with whom I shared my railroad experiences, and as I reached the age of gainful employment, he shared my enthusiasm as I ventured from summer jobs with the Chicago & North Western through my college years, and after two years of teaching, to full-time status at Maine Central.

Alas, he despaired as I reached for advancement, but he was full of stoic advice, much of which I was too impatient to understand at the time, but all of it worthy and correct in retrospect. His counsel prevailed, however, and when I was promoted he shared my excitement and I shared my experiences with him as his health declined. We continued to see each other and correspond right up to the time of his death in 1988.

It was Uncle Dick who in later years pointed to books and boxes full of corporate documents and advised me to look "beyond the pictures," to ask "why" things were; to go beyond the "what" and delve into the "so what?" As a young teenager, I did not always understand, but as I got older and became wiser, the lessons he taught became clear and gained perspective. I'm not sure he ever thought I would someday write books, but perhaps I am selling him short. Maybe, just maybe, he saw in me the potential that I failed to recognize and was laying the groundwork for the day when I would take pen in hand and set to write down what I felt "was important to be recorded—for its own sake." While he was revered and respected by many, he was a lifelong friend and mentor to me, for which my gratitude recognizes no limits. Every boy or girl who likes trains should have an "Uncle Dick."

Wallace Abbey, whose work I have always admired, helped me in the book's initial stages by offering photographs and suggesting leads to photographic material. Over the years he has been a great advisor and a good friend whose help, guidance, and consideration, especially at a time when he was composing his own material, is gratefully appreciated.

A great deal of time and energy was spent by Suzanne Burris, archivist for Burlington Northern Santa Fe. It took her hours to comb through photographs and materials in the BNSF collection on my behalf and this book is richer as a result. Mere words cannot quantify my appreciation for her efforts.

Theodore Shrady also spent hours digging through boxes of research material to find relevant information. In addition, he took time to read through my drafts and offer suggestions for improvement. Without his assistance much of the data contained herein would not have been made available.

Without the capable assistance of Kevin J. Holland, this book would not have the professional appearance that has come to characterize publications such as this. He and I would discuss ideas and he would put them into the layout with his deft sense of proportion and flair for the dramatic.

William F. Howes, Jr., Kevin P. Keefe, and Jack Swanberg helped with the provision of photographs and materials which I have been able to weave into the story. Their generous assistance is gratefully acknowledged.

As is that of John F. Gallagher, Jr. and Herb Harwood, who over the years have been my compasses, pointing me in the direction necessary to tell the story of the railroads and their passenger trains, their stories of success, frustration, and their tales of failure. Beyond respected colleagues, they have become good friends. I am grateful to have been able to draw upon their deep reservoir of knowledge and experience.

I am especially grateful to William Vantuono of Simmons-Boardman Publishing Company for permission to reprint excerpts from the *Railway Age* archives. The magazines proved to be a storehouse of information which accurately documented this important period of railroad history.

Also, I wish to thank Lis Gordon for her assistance in gaining a better understanding about Ralph Budd. Through our conversations she was able to confirm certain aspects about his personality and background, and offered insight into his philosophies.

I am also indebted to Thomas W. Dixon, Jr., my publisher, for allowing me the opportunity to present this story about one of America's greatest and significant fleets of passenger trains. He, too, has been a valuable resource, always turning up some new photograph or forgotten document which seems to have infiltrated his cobweb-festooned vault of railroad files over the decades.

And to William E. Griffin, Jr., Ed Levay, and Mark Reutter for their generosity in lending me items and photographs from their collections, my appreciation for their support.

Andrew Harmantas is the artist who has executed the cover painting, as well as those on my other books. Andrew and I sit in our respective easy chairs and by way of telephonic communication, discuss ideas, letting our fevered imaginations roam, inhibited only by a hint of reality. The result is the striking image that graces the cover of this book. I am envious of his talent and thrilled that he is a collaborator.

To Dana Cayton and Sue Bryer, I owe much as they spent hours transcribing my notes and ramblings. They saved me hours of work which ultimately would have further delayed publication.

To my wife Pamela, my love and gratitude for her understanding and patience. She has come to realize that my books are a labor of love and there are sacrifices to be made in their creation, especially as they come at the expense of some family affairs. Even the dogs seem to understand, resting quietly on the floor while I research and type ... until it's time for dinner.

To you all, my heartfelt thanks for your help and consideration.

PREFACE

When a shiny three-car articulated train called the *Burlington Zephyr* rolled out of the Edward G. Budd Manufacturing Company's plant in Philadelphia on April 7, 1934, only a very few realized that the short train was about to embark on a journey that was destined to herald a new era in train travel across America, and its sleek design was about to have a profound influence on passenger trains over the course of the next fifty years. Furthermore, in a significantly short period of time it would leave an indelible mark on modern train and rail passenger car construction. Although few of the general public grasped the implications of the *Zephyr* at the time, and perhaps even less understood by it today, the new train was more about the future of passenger rail travel and maintaining a market in American transportation than it was an experiment. Indeed, the *Zephyr* was a product of the times, a period in our culture when the manner in which people traveled was experiencing a metamorphosis and when the railroads were becoming engaged in a life and death struggle to retain what was then considered a valued business.

This book is the story of the *Zephyr* era and how the Chicago, Burlington & Quincy Railroad faced the challenges which were being experienced by the railroad passenger industry. The Burlington was an anomaly, however, which makes the story so much more interesting. Unlike the railroads in the eastern region of the country—where the railroads were largely over-built in a highly and densely populated area—much of the Burlington's tracks traversed unpopulated areas and its roster of passenger trains was small when compared to eastern giants New York Central and the Pennsylvania railroads.

In one of the most publicized views of the first *Zephyr*, we see No. 9900 west of Galesburg in June 1934. HAROLD K. VOLLRATH

Excluding its subsidiaries, the Fort Worth & Denver and the Colorado & Southern railroads, the Burlington was likewise small when compared to some of its western neighbors, the Santa Fe, Union Pacific, and its Northern Lines parents, Great Northern and Northern Pacific; thus how it approached the "passenger problem" differed in some respects from these other railroads, and how successful its service ultimately became, contrasted sharply from the level of success experienced by those in the Northeast.

Another related story is to be told about the Pullman/Budd conflict which resulted from the development of the *Burlington Zephyr*, albeit in the form of the *Denver Zephyr* of 1936. The *Denver Zephyr* was the first Burlington train to include stainless steel sleeping cars in its consist and along with the Santa Fe, the railroad became a central player in a legal battle that eventually broke apart a monopoly which Pullman had enjoyed for more than half a century. The outcome of the battle had a tremendous effect on how sleeping car service was delivered in America, but just as important, the court's decision went beyond affecting the Pullman Company and Pullman-Standard—it initiated a chain reaction that altered the railroad industry's delivery of First-Class service in addition to charting the future course of sleeping car manufacturing (see Chapter Five).

This is also a story about the people who brought the *Zephyr* to fruition and who guided its development from the articulated design phase to the more conventional passenger equipment that became so popular in the postwar era. Edward G. Budd, a Philadelphia autobody manufacturer and president of the Budd Company, and Ralph Budd, president of the Burlington, while not related, shared a courageous vision of the future of rail travel. Although drawn together by different motives to be sure, when combined with the talented assistance of Charles Kettering, vice-president of research for General Motors, their vision was brought through to reality due in large part to their determination and conviction that the new train would be successful in addressing the needs of their respective companies and would, indeed, revolutionize the rail industry. Certainly, without the internal combustion engine, the *Zephyr* would never have been created.

For that matter, an argument can be made that were it not for the Great Depression these advances would not have taken place when they did. While it is not entirely true that the railroad industry was unencumbered by progress, it remains a fact that during this time frame the railroads were compelled into making technological improvements by economics and competition, as if driven by the point of a bayonet. This speaks volumes about the industry. Railroads were not known for being proponents of change or innovation, their policies being directed to a large extent by a conservative investment banking industry. Thus, one of the aspects that makes the development of the diesel engine and the *Zephyr* so interesting is that these developments occurred so quickly, in light of the fact that the railroads were so slow to adopt

THE loss of railway passenger traffic during the last decade has been caused by a shifting of travel from the railways to the highway and not from a decline in total travel. In fact, the total passenger one-mile units of travel have greatly increased, but the percentage of the total which has been handled by the railways has been greatly diminished and only twenty per cent as much local traffic by rail was performed in 1933 as in 1920.

Conventional lines have been followed in the design of passenger equipment for a great many years. In departing from convention and undertaking to make improvements that would result in lower train operating costs with added travel comfort, our idea has been to call upon the industry which has taken from us much of our traffic, namely, the automobile industry.

We have accordingly collaborated with the Edward G. Budd Manufacturing Company, the General Motors Corporation and the Massachusetts Institute of Technology, and with two architectural firms, Paul Cret and Holabird & Root. These concerns were given carte blanche in designing and decorating the Zephyr without any restrictions except those which are inherent to railway equipment, namely, the gage of the track and the clearances within which the outside dimensions must be kept.

The railways are very jealous of their record of safety, and stress was laid in our instructions that no compromise be made with safety but that insofar as possible the safety factors must be increased.

In the consideration of material, the character of which must provide the greatest strength with a minimum of weight, it was of paramount importance that we select a material not only uniform in structure, but one entirely non-corrosive to the end that the section which we rely upon and design for may be permanent during the entire service life of the train.

Ralph Budd

radical change—and the diesel *was* radical, if nothing else.

Following in Ralph Budd's footsteps was Harry C. Murphy, who led the Burlington Route during another period of crisis for the railroad industry, the 1950s and 1960s. During the period when the American passenger train was experiencing retrenchment, and when financier and New York Central Chairman Robert R. Young was waging a populist battle to reinvent the passenger train with the introduction of "new trains," or trains of the future, Murphy was ordering conventional stainless steel passenger equipment from the Budd Company to revitalize his railroad's popular *Denver Zephyr*, while pioneering a new type of sleeping car in cooperation with the Budd Company called the "Slumbercoach." The Slumbercoach was a reaction to the trends of the times, but it was successful enough that other railroads bought into the concept and its introduction was to have a modest effect on the shrinking industry. To understand what these individuals were trying to accomplish is to understand the inherent problems of the industry that had to be overcome, and in due course, understand the reasons for the eventual decline of the American passenger train by 1970. This and other stories will appear in the companion volume about the postwar *Zephyrs*.

Still, it is important to recognize that the problems associated with the Northeastern roads, i.e., a decline in the industrial base after the war which left in place a highly populated region with high-cost low-revenue commuter operations, were not altogether shared to the same degree by the Burlington and the western railroads. The West was agrarian in character, and although the Burlington's region was hit hard during the Depression, these important geographical aspects set the western roads apart. Their passenger fleets were proportionate to their demographic operation, and in the case of the distances traveled, the Burlington was losing money on passenger trains in distinct corridors that were tailor-made for the short, articulated, low-cost, diesel-drawn trains—mainly because there was strong potential for regrowth of passenger traffic. All the while the Burlington shared the ill-effects of competition stemming from the growth of federally-funded highways and roads, the growing network of airlines, one-sided regulatory barriers, and nationally-negotiated labor contracts, all of which made the profitable operation of passenger trains so difficult.

And what some may find curious while reading this book is that on the regulatory and subsidy fronts, little has changed. The philosophical battles being waged today are the same—only the dates have been altered.

All these stories are interconnected and make the telling of the *Zephyr* tale more complex. But, it is important to keep in mind that these interwoven stories together made the *Zephyr*s revolutionary as they helped redefine the quality of passenger rail travel by setting new standards for its delivery. Years later, even with advances in air travel technology, our sense of the term "First-Class" would be redefined, cheapened actually, so that its quality would be measured by the dimensions of a slightly wider airline seat. So, these issues must be kept in context, for like any innovation there are reasons for its development, and those reasons say as much about our society as they say about the industry. The *Zephyr's* development was significant for the railroad industry as it shaped the future of the American passenger train, and ultimately influenced its reincarnation through the dawn of a new century.

—*Geoffrey H. Doughty*

"Tomorrow at dawn we'll be on our way."

Ralph Budd
May 25, 1934, on the eve of the non-stop run of the *Zephyr*

BREAK WITH THE PAST

A complaint filed in the Federal District Court of Philadelphia on July 12, 1940, charged that an illegal monopoly existed in the manufacture, ownership, and operation of sleeping cars in the United States. The principal defendants were Pullman, Incorporated, and its two wholly owned subsidiaries, the Pullman-Standard Car Manufacturing Company, the builder of sleeping cars, and the owner-operator of the sleeping car business, the Pullman Company. The suit was brought by the U.S. Justice Department, and although not named as the complainants, the Budd Company, the Chicago, Burlington & Quincy Railroad, and the Atchison, Topeka & Santa Fe Railway were chief among the principals behind the

PARADE OF M

Hig

N

Speed Diesel—Electric Trains

the litigation. The now-famous complaint stemmed from the alleged refusal of the Pullman Company to operate and service the cars of another manufacturer, in this case, the Budd Company. As both the Burlington and the Santa Fe utilized Pullman sleeping cars and had contracts for their operation with Pullman, introduction of sleeping cars made by the rising competitor, Budd, posed a serious threat to Pullman's hegemony in the railroad industry and its future existence. Beginning with the introduction of Budd-built sleeping cars in 1936 in the Burlington's unique *Denver Zephyr* and in Santa Fe's fleet of streamline trains, Pullman intended to discourage their use in any way it could in order to maintain its dominant position. The case would drag on for two years, but with its conclusion all was not settled—it would take another five years for the details to be sorted out and the decision to become effective, and in that five years the railroad industry would be transformed.

Although the Pullman case became a side show and was a by-product of earlier events, the center of attention in 1936 was the introduction of a growing number of new streamline trains in a variety of styles and forms all across the landscape of the American railroad industry. How these trains came to be was a result to a certain degree of what the federal government had been attempting to combat for decades: monopoly. Essentially, the Burlington's marketing plans utilizing articulated trains, coupled with the Budd Company's ingenious construction methods, were attempts to salvage what remained of a once dominant and lucrative market.

BEFORE THE AGE OF THE ZEPHYR

Certainly, monopoly in the railroad industry was nothing new. In fact, the history of the industry would be pretty dull if it were not filled with fascinating tales of wealthy bankers and businessmen locked in corporate combat, thievery, and skulduggery. These nefarious individuals, legendary in the annals of this country's heritage, earned the sobriquet of "Robber Barons," a term and whose legacy would haunt the industry for generations. While it could be pointed out that there were instances when monopolies actually worked well, this didn't matter to a government that felt they should be broken in order to serve the Public Good. In the case of the railroads, monopoly wasn't always a good thing, and as politicians crusaded against the cabals and schemers over time, the result was increasing regulation of the industry. Curiously, however, as far as the strength of the industrial monopoly of transport was concerned, the numerous regulations and the battalions of bureaucratic regulators at both the federal and state levels merely dampened the ill-effects of monopoly rather than reformed it. This situation changed with the development and use of the automobile.

Long before 1920, the rail industry had held a virtual monopoly in transportation, which in the absence of non-rail passenger competition was not necessarily bad. On the other hand, what worked against the benefits of monopoly in this instance was that when it came to the generation of both the passenger and freight businesses, railroads had to do very little in the way of marketing for new traffic. In fact, other than the introduction of the steel passenger car in the early part

One of the earliest attempts made at reducing operating costs on low-density branch lines was the self-propelled railcar. General Electric was one of the first companies to develop a model, with a gasoline-electric power plant. Electro-Motive Company, founded in 1922 and purchased by General Motors in 1930, also built some, as did the Brill Company of Philadelphia. The Burlington amassed one of the largest fleets of these railcars, beginning in 1927. The railroad's subsidiary, Colorado & Southern, used No. 401 in its low-density passenger traffic territory. Combining space for U.S. Mail and baggage/express, cars of this type, called "doodlebugs," helped keep costs in line. *L. C. McCLURE*

of the 20th century, there were few significant innovations in passenger transportation services as such up to 1920. Regardless, passenger-miles increased 206 per cent and railway passenger earnings grew 300 per cent by 1920.[1] There was simply no incentive to try to generate or increase patronage— this might ultimately have had the effect of putting more strain on the railroads and illuminate their shortcomings.

Between 1920 and 1927 a state of stagnation existed. Railroads had passengers knocking down the doors, until the mid 1920s. By 1929, passenger traffic had declined by more than a third to 31 billion passenger-miles, while nobody was looking; earnings on passenger service declined by a third to 874 million dollars, yet revenue per passenger mile was 2.81 cents, as opposed to 2.75 cents in 1920. With revenues up, there was still little incentive to alter their approach. Even though people continued to travel, competition from the other sectors was on the rise and as motor transport technology improved, the ill-effects were soon keenly felt by the railroads.

With the stock market crash of October 29, 1929, the nation's railroads were forced to confront a challenge unlike any which they had met before. Freight traffic, the bread and butter of a railroad, fell precipitously. So did passenger traffic. Although much passenger service was mandated by regulation, up to this point in time it was still profitable. While passenger service added considerable revenue to the railroads' bottom line, by 1930 the decline in passenger traffic was accelerating, so much so that by 1933 passenger-miles were two-thirds that of the level in 1920; total earnings from passenger service were just three-fourths of what they had been in 1920; and earnings per train-mile were just $1.28, less than half of that in 1920.

At the beginning of 1933, the Great Depression had been underway for three years and two months, and on a cold March 4 of that year, a new president, Franklin Delano Roosevelt, took the oath of office in the midst of what was by then this nation's worst economic crisis in its history. What Roosevelt offered was hope in a land which was obsessed with its plight. The banks were closed, industry was all but shut down, and millions were out of work. Government, he maintained, would have to offer the American public a "New Deal," and it would come in the form of more government involvement in the economy. What was unknown at the time was that the railroad industry would play a pivotal role in helping lead the country out of its doldrums. That year, 1933, would be the low point of the crisis, and although there would be ripples of recession during the next five years, the society—and its railroads—would prove to be resilient.

THE GREAT DEPRESSION — CATALYST FOR CHANGE

In its incipient stages, the Depression created serious and widespread economic deprivations for millions who were without gainful employment. Although the Hoover Administration had taken very modest steps to help American industry, three years were to elapse before the federal government took more robust efforts to intervene during the early days of the Roosevelt Administration. Through government-sponsored programs the federal government stepped up its efforts to aid those industries that could promote and create employment, and although the rail and its supply industry were two of the country's leading employers, it would be the building of roads and other massive public works projects that would put people back to work. Significantly, throughout the decade of the 1930s, forms of alternative transportation made rapid advances in popularity capitalizing on the help from the governmental sector.

The population, meanwhile, focused inward on its troubles, escaping to diversions, away from daily and mundane lives. Radio, which by then had become a fixture in the American home, brought Americans a focal point of evening activity. Much like the technology of the telephone, it was a form of communication. President Roosevelt deftly used the medium to communicate with the troubled nation in his "fireside chats," an attempt to become more familiar to the electorate and to engender the feeling of a compassionate friend who would lead them through the crisis. Music, heretofore heard only in concert halls and in parks on Sunday afternoons, now could be heard in the home from the box in the living room, as music acquired an important

Every day, American's luxurious skysleepers carry scores of passengers across the nation on its famous Southern Sunshine Route. First two, then three, then four—and now *five* American Airlines flights daily each way from coast-to-coast are required to meet public demand.

This nature-favored airway connects New York and Los Angeles in one smooth overnight flight over Virginia, Tennessee and the colorful Sun Country of Texas and Arizona. It links vitally important centers of commerce and industry. It provides bustling Washington, D. C. with quick transcontinental service.

The Southern Sunshine Route is preferred by air travelers not only for smooth, comfortable flight but also because American flies it! That means courteous, thoughtful attention from the staff on the ground, the crew in the air; the comfort and convenience of the modern Flagship; the many ingenious ways American has devised to make even the briefest journeys superbly enjoyable. Enjoy your next trip to the fullest—*Go American!* Call your Travel Agent or the nearest American Airlines office.

Send for beautiful full-color Sun Country booklet. (Enclose 10c coin or stamps for postage and handling.) Dept. 25, American Airlines, Inc., Jackson Heights, N. Y.

AMERICAN AIRLINES *Inc.*
ROUTE OF THE FLAGSHIPS

In the 1930s, fledgling airlines began to attract long-distance passengers away from America's railroads. The 1936 introduction of the Douglas DC-3 was a watershed event for the airlines—*and* the railroads.
KEVIN J. HOLLAND COLLECTION

role in soothing and distracting the populace from their problems. Classical music, ever popular during this period, was being conducted by world-renowned orchestral conductors such as Arturo Toscanini, who was leading the New York Philharmonic in performances (1929–1936), and in 1937 began performing weekly nationally broadcast concerts as conductor of the celebrated NBC Symphony Orchestra—a radio orchestra created by David Sarnoff of RCA especially for Toscanini. With the development of the then-modern record player (which spun flat hard rubber discs on a turntable at 78 rpm), Toscanini and his contemporaries Frederick Stock at the Chicago Symphony, Serge Koussevitzky with the Boston Symphony Orchestra, and Leopold Stokowski and his successor Eugene Ormandy leading the Philadelphia Orchestra, had been making recordings for RCA Victor and Decca Records, which personalized musical taste, provid-

ing it on demand for a mass market. Although record production came to a near standstill in the early years of the Depression, the ease with which this type of personal technology was made accessible was making life easier and more enjoyable when the public desperately needed a distraction.

The populace became captivated by the styles of the times, entranced by innovation, indulging and immersing themselves in the galaxies of the movies, sports, opera, and famous personalities. Just a few years before the world had entered the age of the "talkies," another giant leap in technology. Entertainment became one of the great escapes, as did following the lives of the rich and the famous. While many Americans had to do without, they still could dream.

Aviators, too, became instant celebrities while attempting new records in flight. Charles Lindbergh and Amelia Earhart captured the headlines by flying greater distances than were ever thought possible. In 1932, after having obtained lucrative mail contracts from the United States Post Office Department, Transcontinental & Western Air, the predecessor to Trans World Airlines, requested a design for a dual-engine 12-passenger airplane from Douglas Aircraft, which produced its DC-1, delivered in December 1933. Although only one example was built, it was followed quickly by the DC-2 which could carry 14 passengers, and the DC-3 which carried 21. The new airplanes entered service in 1934 and 1936 respectively, and could fly at a cruising speed of 150 mph. Speed became of ever increasing importance as technology made higher limits possible, but flying was anything but a refined mode of transport. Passengers on the early Ford Tri-Motor airplane, for example, were provided with grab handles on the backs of the seat in front of them as the seats weren't equipped with seatbelts. Still in their infancy, the fledgling airlines, what few there were, had to contend with bad weather, schedule delays, cancellations, cold cabins, uncomfortable rides, and the lack of certain amenities, such as flush toilets. Even more primitive than those on trains, the latter time-honored method would have shocked today's environmentalists.

To a cultured society, fashion and style also became of increasing importance. If anything, the 1930s will be remembered as the period of the Art Deco movement, and everything imaginable reflected its influence, from lamps, radios, and furnishings, to automobiles. Chrysler introduced its "Airflow" model in 1934, the first mass-produced streamlined automobile. In the field of architecture, the Art Deco movement would find its most stunning outlet as each city had buildings which reflected the artistic movement's influence. The Chrysler Building, with its ornate peak and spire, designed by William van Alen, became one of New York City's most famous landmarks (1930). A year later the Empire State Building opened, then the world's tallest at 102 stories.

Streamlining was an Art Deco movement by-product, with its general style of curves and bright colors, and the Burlington was soon to take advantage of it. In the Northeast, railroads with extensive rail passenger services such as the New York Central, Pennsylvania, and the New Haven, were acutely aware that if their services were to be attractive to the public they had to appear in touch with the times by appealing to the public's sensitive aesthetic tastes. Simply put, they had to make traveling by train popular again, and recognizing the importance that style played in the public's spending habits, it was imperative that they make their patrons feel as though they were traveling "in style." To accomplish this the railroads turned to famous industrial designers to help them (men like Henry Dreyfus, Raymond Loewy, Otto Kuhler, and Walter Dorwin Teague), but only after the introduction of the *Zephyr*.

The factors of diversions, the increasing use of radio, the focus on style, the introduction of the Art Deco period, and the advent of personal technology, all came together as the railroad industry struggled to find its way out of the abyss of revenue deprivation.

In 1933, the state of affairs within the railroad industry mirrored that of the country. The portrait being painted was gloomy. Although rail passenger transportation remained the dominant form of long-distance transport, the popularity and use of intercity passenger trains had already peaked by 1929. Even still, incredibly, there were only a few within the industry who recognized that the railroads' monopoly in ground transport was nearing

an end, as automobiles, trucks, and buses gradually, but steadily, eroded rail's market dominance. Meanwhile, an infant airline industry had been quietly gaining in popularity. In fact, since 1925, the federal government had been pouring massive amounts of funds into the improvement of airports and facilities, and airline use expanded exponentially from one million passenger-miles in 1926 to 95 million in 1930. By 1936 it would rise to 439 million.

Adding to this disturbing trend, at least from the railroads' point of view, was the fact that the automobile and trucking industries were being aided by their allies in government at both the state and federal levels, an alliance that had its origins in the first federal omnibus transportation (i.e., highway) bill in 1916. By 1930 there were approximately 660,000 miles of highways, handling ten times as many passenger-miles as the railroads. America was still on the move, but now by other means to the exclusion of rail.

In the late 1930s, Detroit was also combining mythology and mobility. *KEVIN J. HOLLAND COLLECTION*

Thus, the Great Depression brought many railroads their greatest financial losses since the end of World War I, just 11 years before, and for many bankruptcy became the measure of last resort. The rail industry was particularly hard hit, and as the economic crisis deepened, it only exacerbated a poor situation.

Despite hardships and vast unemployment, the period of the Depression became a peculiar catalyst for change as industries struggled to find new and innovative ways to cut costs, become more efficient, and attract new business. These innovations did not occur in a vacuum, however. In many ways the changes in the American culture were the result of improved technology, and as technology matured so then did the culture evolve. It was a revolving cycle of change, improvement, and more change. Furthermore, it is imperative to note that the changes that were occurring in the rail industry, and in the nation as a whole, were taking place during a period when the economy was at its worst, not when it was at its best. Although government was playing more of a role in the lives of the American public and was actively helping to extricate industry from the worsening economic situation, it was competition among industries that was the critical factor in the development of the new types of metallurgy and improved rail service, not governmental intervention.

Another significant factor was the act of saving time, and in retrospect the nation was becoming obsessed with it. Paved roads, combined with the accessability and affordable cost of the automobile, altered spacial relationships. Improved communications during this period altered those relationships as well, which had the added beneficial effect of aiding commerce. With the growing availability of airline service throughout the 1930s, transit times between distant cities could be greatly reduced, despite the occasional inconvenience of weather and/or mechanical delays. The public would slowly become acclimated to such matters and would be willing to sacrifice the comforts of train travel for the mediocrity associated with air and automobile travel in the interest of convenience.

The railroads during this period were quick to recognize the preference of a public that wanted to make better use of time, so speed of transit became an issue and had to be improved upon in order for the railroads to remain competitive. Thus, they would capitalize on the convenience, comfort, and relative speed of their passenger trains which was still faster than any car could safely travel, and with airplanes only able to cruise at 150 mph within a limited range, the train was a viable competitor.

Regardless, by 1930 the railroads saw trouble ahead and they realized that they had to act if they were to remain in the passenger business, but their options were limited.* Railroads, tightly regulated by the Interstate Commerce Commission and many state regulatory bodies, or public utilities commissions, had little room to alter the status quo of operations, so eliminating services or reducing employment was not always a viable alternative. These agencies imposed strict requirements upon the railroads to operate passenger trains even if only to maintain a level of service in the face of declining patronage. The railroads needed relief, and if they couldn't get it at the regulatory and labor contractual levels, then they had to seek other alternatives to reduce costs while attracting new business, something they had previously not had to do. They suddenly found themselves fighting to retain the business they had. Two alternatives of which the railroads could still take advantage were improvements in train and car design. Fortunately for the railroads, a coincidence of events was taking place.

NEW TRAINS

The timing of the search for new types of equipment came at the moment when there was intensive on-going research, development, and experimentation of new lightweight metallurgy and interest in its utilization in train and car design. Since 1929, railroad car manufacturers had been experimenting with steel alloys, such as aluminum, and to a lesser extent stainless steel, whose attribute of reduced weight improved fuel economy and lowered maintenance costs by reducing wear on equipment, track, and roadbeds. When combined with the element of streamlining, the lighter weight of the passenger cars allowed greater speeds of trains and, therefore, better transit times between stations. Later, as the

*During the Depression years leading up to the war, for example, railroad passenger-miles increased only eight percent, while bus passenger-miles increased 100 percent, almost doubling since 1930, increasing from 11.2 billion to 21 billion. During the same period, air passenger-miles increased a total of 711 percent. Meanwhile, the number of automobiles registered grew from 22,972,745 in 1930 to 27,372,397 in 1940.

rolling resistance of passenger cars improved through the use of new roller bearing technology, lighter and less costly locomotives could be employed to pull them, thus further reducing wear. Also, lighter locomotives increased fuel economy, allowing for greater utilization of the cars and engines on branch lines and obtaining a lower operating cost per passenger-mile.

Both aluminum and stainless steel had their individual merits. They had non-corrosive characteristics and they did not require painting. Their tensile strength was approximately three times greater than carbon steel, then commonly used in railroad car manufacturing, although it was of almost equal weight. Aluminum was being used by several manufacturers, most notable among them Pullman-Standard which was experimenting with the metal in some of its period passenger cars. The use of aluminum in passenger car construction saved approximately 50 percent in car weight.

Meanwhile, the Edward G. Budd Manufacturing Company had developed a unique "Shotweld" process using electrical current to effect the welds necessary in stainless steel construction, yet the procedure did not break down the surface of the metal, allowing it to remain corrosion-resistant. Stainless steel's cost, however, was much greater than ordinary steel, which for many railroads became a mitigating factor. Whereas a pound of carbon steel cost two or three cents, a pound of aluminum and stainless steel cost 35 cents. The relative savings of both types of construction were to be found in the factors of their high tensile strength and the amount of either metal necessary in the overall production process. Further economies could be found in the replacement of interior appointments, such as in seat design, manufactured with lighter weight materials such as aluminum. Ultimately, however, stainless steel proved to be more popular for train construction while aluminum was used for interior appointments.

Another important innovation was that of the articulated train. Articulated trains went another step beyond car design by reducing overall train weight, and reducing friction through improved truck design and a reduction in the number of trucks necessary for the train. This technological advance also resulted in reduced cost of maintenance, but also improved riding qualities as the articulated design eliminated the slack action found between separate passenger cars. While not commonly employed in 1930, it caught the attention of those few visionaries within the rail industry, such as Ralph Budd.

The year 1933 was an important one for American railroads. By that time, this country's steel alloy industry was marketing new products under various trade names, and there were experiments in new types of mechanical locomotion, such as diesels and petroleum distillate engines. Pullman-Standard had been in the development phase of a new type of self-propelled car, called the "Railplane," utilizing one of the new alloys, called "Duralumin," a heat-treated aluminum alloy containing the strength of structural steel, but with a fraction of the weight. The *Railplane* unit was 60 feet long, could seat 50 passengers, and was designed to operate at speeds of about 90 mph. Its very name seemed to play on the public's fascination with air flight.

Built of welded tubular steel and covered in aluminum sheeting, it was propelled by a pair of 160-hp Waukesha six-cylinder automobile engines. These two motors were ingeniously mounted on either side of the front truck between the

Pullman's lightweight railcar, called "Railplane," was designed to operate at speeds of about 90 mph. While it did catch attention, no sales resulted. This is the front-end view of the *Railplane* which details the streamlined body and unique buffer plate. The car was designed to operate by itself rather than in pairs, and only one example was built. *RAILWAY AGE*

The *Railplane* was powered by two Waukesha six-cylinder automotive engines. These developed 160-hp each at a speed of 2,200 rpm. Mounted on either side of the front truck, the engines utilized the space between the outside of the wheels and the outside of the carbody, which made them accessible for servicing. The carbody of the *Railplane* was framed with welded tubular steel. It was determined that at a top speed of 90 mph the wind resistance for the *Railplane* could be reduced by more than 50% by proper streamlining. *Railway Age*

*The Brill Company—in 1932, a leading supplier of electric rail transit motorcars—came up with a design for a new high-speed model as well. It could seat 52 passengers and travel at 70 mph, but sales were limited as the railroad traction market was shrinking.

axles, hung on the outside of the truck frame. One engine drove the front axle while the other drove the rear, utilizing a specially designed Banker clutch, universal joint, and gear transmission, manufactured by the Timken-Detroit Axle Company. Timken also furnished the wheels and roller bearings.

After extensive research and testing, Pullman-Standard determined that at 90 mph on straight level track, the wind resistance for the conventional passenger car design was 90 percent of total resistance, and that this amount could be reduced by half when combined with the element of streamlining. Wind tunnel and wind resistance testing became an important factor in increasing train speeds, and eventually influencing train design. The *Railplane* looked much like a hot dog and although it was successful in raising eyebrows, no sales resulted.*

Pullman-Standard would find success a year later with their entry, Union Pacif-

ic's M-10000 articulated train, also made of aluminum. In a race with the Burlington/Budd combination, their train was powered by a 600-hp distillate-electric power plant. The three-coach train was capable of reaching a speed of 110 mph. The train's cost was $200,000 and was built with the conviction that in order to rescue the declining passenger train business, radical measures in train design were necessary.[2]

The Budd Company, meanwhile, which held the patent for its Shotweld process, had already built and marketed several new lightweight stainless steel passenger cars and trains. In 1931, for example, in cooperation with Michelin, the French tire manufacturer, Budd unveiled its Budd-Michelin Experimental Car which had a top speed of 40 mph, could carry 40 passengers, and was operated with an electric drive with a two-cycle diesel engine. Its wheels were specially designed utilizing pneumatic tires for a quieter ride. Although few sales resulted and it was generally unsuccessful in operation, it paved the way to other experiments, such as the Reading Railroad's 47-seat railcar driven by a four-cycle Cummins diesel, also with pneumatic tires, which could reach a top speed of 50 mph—on dry rails.

For the Pennsylvania, Budd built a two-car stainless steel train in 1931 that had a capacity of 76 passengers, and contained space for baggage and express as well as toilet facilities. Also driven by a four-cycle Cummins diesel engine and riding on pneumatic tires, the train could reach a top speed of 60 mph, but once again its success in service was marginal.

On October 24, 1933, another rubber-tired train rolled out of Budd's plant, this one built for the Texas & Pacific. The train, test run in the Burlington's Chicago suburban territory, operated on a seven-day round trip schedule between Fort Worth and Texarkana, Arkansas, a distance of about 500 miles. Its delivery made it the first completely equipped stainless steel lightweight train to be placed in long-distance main line service. Its general design, while boxy, was a glimpse of what would follow. Built of stainless steel, the power car contained two 240-hp, 12-cylinder American-La France gasoline engines, housed at the very front of the car and connected to Westinghouse main and auxiliary generators. A 15-foot Railway Post Office (RPO) compartment and a 33-foot baggage and express section was also included. A trailer car containing three passenger compartments completed the set.

The contemporary description of the train's passenger section is a lesson in period culturalism.

The second car of the train is devoted entirely to passenger accommodations. At the front end is a 12-foot compartment for colored passengers, with seats for 16. Immediately behind this are two lavatories, one on either side of the car. One of these, for colored passengers, opens into the front passenger compartment. The other, for white passengers, opens onto a short corridor just forward of the entrance vestibule. In the rear of the vestibule is the 35-foot main passenger compartment which seats 48 passengers. At the rear of the car is a smoking observation compartment with seats for 12.[3]

This was, after all, the 1930s and the Texas & Pacific operated in prime southern territory.

Although it had its faults, the Texas & Pacific's Budd-built lightweight two-car gas-electric "Silver Slipper" train became the first completely equipped passenger train built of stainless steel to be placed in long-distance mainline service. Only one example was built, but at the time that the Burlington was ordering its first *Zephyr*, the T&P train was already under construction. The stainless steel fluting on its sides set a standard which was to be repeated with the Burlington train. The T&P train was tested on the Burlington's Chicago suburban lines in late October 1933. The train's power plant and Railway Post Office, along with space for baggage and express, were located in the first unit. Power was supplied by a pair of 240-horsepower American-La France gasoline engines connected to Westinghouse main and auxiliary generators. The nose had doors to facilitate the removal of the engine's generating unit. The passenger coach was supported and carried by trucks composed of stainless steel frames with eight Budd pneumatic-tired wheels in each truck, fitted with Timken bearings. The Goodyear tires, designed by Michelin, were intended to provide a quieter and smoother ride, but the train suffered problems in their use. The baggage compartment contained the heating and air conditioning equipment. The low-pressure steam boiler was furnished by the Vapor Car Heating Company. *ALL, RAILWAY AGE*

Streamlining was a by-product of the Art Deco period. At first, many railroads streamlined some of their locomotives in order to take advantage of current cultural trends. The Union Pacific Railroad was a leader in the field of streamlining, placing a streamlined shroud over engine No. 7002 as an example. New York Central was another. The Burlington would emulate the practice in 1936. *Otto Perry, Denver Public Library Western History Department*

Union Pacific's streamlined No. 7002 was photographed at speed in the 1930s, pulling a decidedly unstreamlined Overland Route train. *TLC Collection*

This new train from Budd had a cruising speed of 75 mph and was expected to operate at approximately half the cost of a steam-driven train.

Budd's advertising claims stated that the system of stainless steel construction reduced wind resistance and the lighter weight furthered the train's operating efficiency and economy. Unfortunately, the train proved to be unreliable and suffered from numerous failures of one type or another, and although the pneumatic tires seemed to be a great idea and were placed only on the trailer wheels instead

of the drive wheels, failure continued to plague the design when used in regular service.

All of these trains were experiments, since few were being built in numbers, yet when combined with diesel technology they seemed to hold great potential if produced with standard steel wheels. Efficiency and economy were great attractions and these were just two of the trains' attributes which interested the executives at the Chicago, Burlington & Quincy. The others were speed, comfort, and their ability to attract passengers. ■

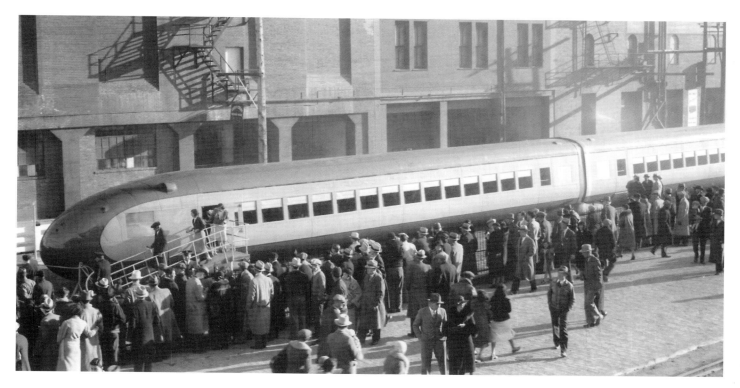

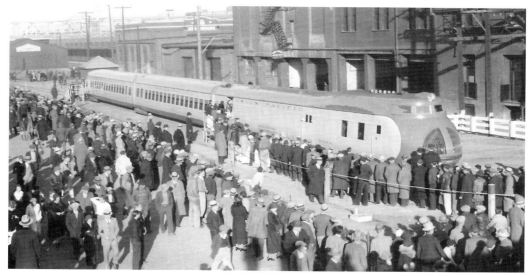

Union Pacific's M-10000 is seen as it was placed on display in Denver in 1934. During its publicity tour, the public got a chance to take a glimpse of the future. Initially, the M-10000 consisted of three lightweight carbodies, a power car driven by a distillate engine, containing a section for baggage and mail sorting, and two passenger coaches. Originally intended to be powered by a Model 201A diesel engine built by Winton, this engine had not yet then been perfected, so the distillate-powered unit was substituted in the race to be the "first" streamlined train in the West to be powered by an internal-combustion engine. The M-10000's observation car was "worm-like" in design, and did not afford a view behind the train. This design was intended to reduce air drag, but it did nothing in the way of passenger enjoyment. It did not take Pullman long to figure this out. *BOTH, OTTO PERRY, DENVER PUBLIC LIBRARY WESTERN HISTORY DEPARTMENT*

bottom: The Union Pacific expanded the M-10000 to a four-car train and placed it on display at the Century of Progress Exhibition being held in Chicago where it attracted a great deal of attention from the public. *OTTO PERRY, DENVER PUBLIC LIBRARY WESTERN HISTORY DEPARTMENT*

2 LOOKING TO THE FUTURE

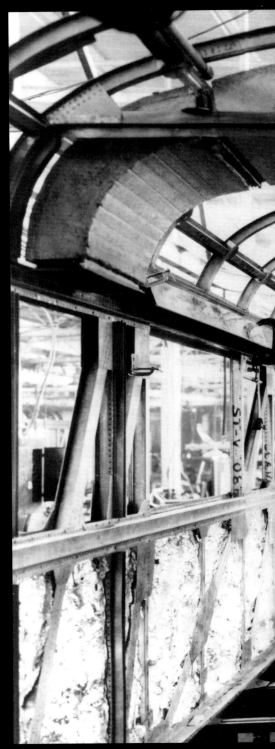

The Chicago, Burlington & Quincy Railroad of the 1930s reflected decades of growth and change. The company was controlled by the Northern Pacific and the Great Northern, and in turn the Burlington controlled the Colorado & Southern and the Fort Worth & Denver. Operating in 14 states and over approximately 11,000 miles of track, the Burlington ran as far north as Minneapolis, Minnesota, as far west as Denver, Colorado, and through its aforementioned subsidiaries, as far south as Galveston, Texas. Its easternmost terminal was Chicago, from which its major and most famous trains departed. Through its connections with its owners, the Burlington had access to the Pacific Northwest.

We are inside the observation car of the *Burlington Zephyr*. Taken in February 1934, this view shows that the car's air-conditioning duct has been installed overhead and the insulation is being applied. Apparently, much work remains to be done. *BOMBARDIER CORPORATION, MARK REUTTER COLLECTION*

Ralph Budd. *BNSF ARCHIVES*

*Budd was an early advocate of the nation's railroads being consolidated into a limited number of railway systems. He strongly believed that consolidation of rail lines was in the public interest and would eliminate waste and improve efficiency in a variety of sectors. The Northern Lines, which owned 97 percent of Burlington stock, had put their case before the ICC as far back as 1901, yet it took 69 years before it was effected—and that's another story.

Its most popular passenger trains from Chicago traveled its mainline routes to the Twin Cities and to Denver. Until the Great Depression, shorter runs between Omaha, Kansas City, and St. Louis also provided the railroad with substantial passenger traffic. For its overnight traffic, the Burlington, like most railroads that operated overnight trains, contracted with the Pullman Company to provide sleeping car service on its premier trains, the *Aristocrat* and the *Exposition Flyer*, among others.

The railroad's president was Ralph Budd. Although he was endowed with considerable engineering and railroad experience, nothing seemed as formidable a challenge as the Great Depression. When he assumed office on January 1, 1932, the country had not yet even reached the low point of the unprecedented economic crisis.

Budd succeeded Frederic E. Williamson, who had resigned to become president of New York Central. Since 1916, he had been a director of the Chicago, Burlington & Quincy, and from 1919 he had been president of the Great Northern. Born to a conservative family of farmers near Waterloo, Iowa, in 1879, he grew up appreciating the advantages of a good education. By the time he entered Highland Park College in Des Moines, Iowa, he was already an avid reader of the classics, from prose to poetry. He also became a

student of history with a thorough grasp of detail, an attribute which was to become an integral part of his character for the rest of his life and which would hold him in good stead during the career that he was about to undertake. He graduated from Highland Park College with a bachelor's degree in civil engineering in 1899, and from there he became a draftsman employed by the Chicago Great Western, where in 1900 he became assistant engineer.

A significant turning point in Budd's life occurred when in 1902 he was offered a job at the Rock Island Railroad. There he went to work for John F. Stevens, becoming division engineer in 1903. Although Stevens left the railroad to work on the Panama Canal Railroad project, in 1906 he called Budd and offered him a job. Budd accepted, and there he earned more engineering experience and a reputation for innovation. When Stevens went to work for the Oregon Trunk in 1909, Ralph Budd followed. In 1910, Budd was promoted to chief engineer of the Oregon Trunk, and shortly thereafter, became chief engineer of the Spokane, Portland & Seattle Railroad.

In 1912, railroad magnate James Hill asked Budd to become assistant to the president of the Great Northern, where he was later promoted to chief engineer, and then in 1918, to executive vice-president. At age 40, a seasoned and experienced railroader, he was elected president of Great Northern in 1919. Among his many accomplishments there, Budd oversaw the building of the Cascade Tunnel in Washington State, and between 1927 and 1929 he began to lay the foundations for what would ultimately result in the merger of the Great Northern, the Northern Pacific, and the Chicago, Burlington & Quincy railroads.*

A quiet, educated, and singularly modest gentleman, Budd did not fit the historical mold of the archetypical railroad official. Polite, courteous, and with an engaging personality, he looked more like a university professor than a chief executive of a railroad. A voracious learner, he could not travel his railroad without inquiring about over which river or creek his train was operating, or what specie of flora was most evident. One close advisor stated, "Traveling with Budd was something like taking an escorted tour with a naturalist."[4] As a leader, he was to prove adroit and proficient, with an atypical sense of perspective, equaled only by his sense of humanity. For many, Budd was the right man for the job.

By the end of January 1932, the net railway operating income of the Burlington had fallen 72 percent from that in 1931. All of industry was adversely affected, and although from the outset government was slow to react, there was movement to try to stem the tide of effects from the crisis. On January 22, 1932, President Herbert Hoover had signed legislation to establish the Reconstruction Finance Corporation, which acted as a giant lending institution to American industry and its railroads. Organized labor, recognizing the threat the economic crisis posed to its membership, agreed to a ten percent wage reduction on February 1, 1932, in the hopes that this would ease the burden on the railroads and slow the rate of layoffs. While this was helpful to an extent, the fact remained that wage rates, taxes, and interest on funded debt remained unchanged since the peak years of prosperity and produced a serious financial strain on America's railroads.

With the Depression deepening, these remedial measures by themselves had no effect on the decline in freight car loadings, which in 1932 were off by 25 percent from the year before. Likewise, passenger revenue had fallen 34.75 percent from that in 1931. Net railway income had fallen from a high of $26 million in 1928 to $1,502,816.

Budd knew that savings could be found in improved engineering, mechanics, and safety. Improvements to track and roadbed, through reduction of grades and curves (elevation), and increases in car capacity and train size, in addition to the introduction of lighter materials in the production of cars and locomotives, would ease ton-mile costs. Increased emphasis on safety would result in less personal injury and property loss. By increasing efficiency, the railroad would be better able to confront the competition of the trucks and automobile head-on.

Yet, he was also astute enough to recognize that increasing efficiency and eliminating waste would not reverse the losses the Burlington was experiencing. The railroad could not save its way to prosperity. While he and his managers identified the expense issues, they also realized they had to address the revenue issues. Budd knew that there was not much more freight traffic to be had in the region that the Burlington operated, and surrounded by larger roads, the Burlington was left to fight for whatever scraps of freight traffic were left. Although the Burlington held the distinction of being the only railroad to operate over its own rails between Chicago and Denver, this was not enough to beat the competition—the challenge of operating in the land of the giants would put to the test the talents of the best of managers. He had to look elsewhere for new opportunities.

Budd realized that within this environment, the one area that did hold some potential for growth was passenger traffic. Fully aware of the competition of the improving highways, and the increasing influence of the highway/automobile industries in Washington, he reasoned that a new fast train, if it could be built, might just draw traffic back to the rails.

In the years just before the Depression, the Burlington had tried self-propelled gas-electric motor cars, or "doodlebugs," and although they were economical, their passenger capacity and speed were limited. Budd's idea of a new train was that it had to be air-conditioned, clean, comfortable, and had to be of lighter weight in order for it to reduce transit times and, thus, be attractive to passengers and become profitable. Unfortunately, the technology of 1932 did not lend itself to an easy solution, but his ideas were not his alone.

Within the next few years, other railroads, such as neighbor Union Pacific, under the leadership of Edward Harriman, and in the Northeast at the New Haven Railroad under Howard Palmer, thoughts of regaining passenger traffic and finding solutions for shrinking market share and addressing the regulatory climate were heading in the same direction. Harriman felt that drastic times called for bold measures, especially in train design, if the situation was to be turned around. By the time Palmer became president in late 1934, he recognized that his railroad had no choice but to keep investing in new modern equipment because of an aging passenger fleet and the vital need to retain passenger traffic which accounted for over 40 percent of the New Haven's revenues. He also had to straighten out decades of tangled financial schemes to turn his railroad into a revenue producer. Passenger car and train design were instrumental in that railroad's recovery.

Ralph Budd was fortunate in that during the period of the prosperous 1920s, the railroads in general had made considerable improvements to their physical plants and had increased their efficiency and expanded their capacity to handle freight and passenger traffic. So had the Burlington. Yet, as investment increased, so did the tax burden. Coincidentally, this expansion and improvement, which had cost the railroads an estimated $6 billion, had taken place at the same time of the massive investment in highways by the federal and state governments. When rail's freight traffic fell dramatically in 1930, the railroads were left with expensive physical plants and overhead expenses that could not be readily reduced by railway managements. So, governmental intervention by way of subsidizing rail's competition (including waterways) did not bode well for the future of the railroads. To make matters worse, legislation being passed that set its sights at regulating the rail industry assumed that the railroads still held a monopoly in transportation. While there once had been a time when it might have been appropriate, it was no longer the case.

Here Ralph Budd had to find his way through a morass of interconnected issues in order to improve his company's financial situation, especially if a new train as he envisioned were to be successful. Budd was one who strongly believed that each mode of transport retained certain inherent advantages and, therefore, should be allowed to serve those markets where their advantages worked best.* But, other modes were yet to come under federal regulation. He felt that all transportation should be regulated in the public interest, with governmental intervention only when necessary, with no one competitor being given an unfair advantage. On numerous occasions he spoke out against the ills of over-regulation and focusing on one industry—the railroads. Legislation, he said, should not raise the costs of operation. Unfortunately, this theory ultimately seemed lost on legislators and regulators.

One very real threat posed by the economic situation that would affect both labor and management was that of government ownership of the railroads. With much of the railroad industry entering bankruptcy, government ownership of the country's railroads was a serious matter, and many outside the industry saw it as a viable option. Budd didn't mince his words about the possibility, saying that such a move would increase costs, lower productivity, and worsen service. Government ownership might evolve if the fortunes of the industry did not improve, and with that thought in mind, further regulation of the industry would only make matters worse. He pointed to the Emergency Transportation Act of 1933 as a prime example, since it severely restricted the ability of the railroads to reduce costs by eliminating jobs. The train limit bill, "full crew" laws, and the bill that provided for a six-hour period to calculate a day's pay, were proof positive that government ownership would increase the cost of transportation. Imposing these same restrictions on the privately-owned railroads would make it impossible to compete unless similar legislation were enacted and imposed on rail's competitors.[5]

One solution that Budd promoted was the consolidation of approximately 850 of the country's railroads into about 20 companies. Such a move would remove unprofitable routes, save the most favorable, reduce redundant employment, reduce overhead costs, improve terminal operations, and foster efficiency. While such an action would present political and logistical problems, these, Budd believed, would be short-term. The fact that this would mean the elimination of jobs during the consolidation process was bound to create a monstrous controversy, and vociferous opposition, but it was a solution which could not be overlooked.**

Thus, the matter of labor relations was of utmost concern for the Burlington's new president. Even by Depression standards, labor costs were expensive. The railroad industry was locked into agreements that had been formulated in a bygone era, and which did not account for technological advances that would improve efficiency and promote economy. The unions were adamant that they

*Indeed, this was codified in the Emergency Transportation Act of 1933, which also created a position of a federal "transportation coordinator" who was granted authority to root out waste, eliminate duplicated services and preventable expense. But, there was a catch—any economies should not come at the expense of labor in the form of layoffs. The last thing the government wanted was more unemployment.

**Consolidation of railroads was relatively new. The Transportation Act of 1920 enabled railroads for the first time to merge in order to effect certain economies of operation, while ensuring the preservation of competition.

Edward G. Budd pioneered the "Shotweld" process, in which extremely high voltage was used to effect a weld which did not break down the strength of metal. If made with traditional welding methods using oxyacetylene, stainless steel broke down. Edward Budd and his engineering staff developed the spot-weld technique which eliminated the use of other materials to effect the welds. While the process was patented by Budd, what is generally not known is that the company did offer the technology later to its biggest competitor, Pullman-Standard, but was turned down. *BNSF ARCHIVES*

should not give up privileges, accept lower wages, or change work rules so that the railroads could control costs, despite the fact that labor's wages were consuming more than half the revenues of the railroads. Such an approach, Budd countered, would end up in fewer union jobs and eventual bankruptcy for their employers.

Meanwhile, state and federal regulators, heavily influenced by organized labor, continued to determine what regulations were imposed and what actions the railroads could take to reduce costs, including limiting reductions in the workforce. Therefore, whatever solution was to be found in a new train would have to take into account the cost of labor and the trend of the railroad passenger car indus-

try toward making heavier and more expensive equipment, which in turn increased maintenance costs.

It was within this complicated multifaceted environment that Ralph Budd traveled to Philadelphia on September 29, 1932, to ride a gas-electric car at Edward Budd's plant, in search of a solution to the declining passenger market. One of the car's attributes which intrigued Ralph Budd was the Shotweld process that the elder Budd had developed.

Perceptively, Ralph Budd foresaw the importance of the ability of trains to move faster and was thus drawn to the Budd Company's emphasis on streamlining its railway products. Here, both Budds would be utilizing the theories of aerodynamics with new construction techniques and materials to win back passengers. The two, both with engineering backgrounds, saw in each other great potential for improving their own business.

Impressed with what he saw at the Budd Company plant, Ralph Budd made arrangements for the railroad to order a three-car articulated train shortly after his return from Philadelphia. Yet, the question still without an answer was how the train would be powered. Previous experiments had not been unqualified successes. A year was to pass before a solution would be found.

With the inauguration of Franklin Roosevelt in March 1933, the low point of the Depression was at hand. For the Burlington, the added governmental support for America's farmers eased the burden on the average farm family. Within the next few years, the numerous building projects and newly formed governmental agencies that were designed to encourage employment and public works projects,

ultimately fueled a demand for farm products. Likewise, the building projects resulted in an increase in manufactured goods and forest products. Even still, these developments were not enough to improve the Burlington's financial position substantially as traffic remained at historically low levels.

Regardless, Budd's dream of placing his new streamlined train in service was drawing near. In Detroit, engineers at General Motors' Electro-Motive Corporation (EMC) and at Winton Engine Company, under the combined direction of Charles F. Kettering, vice-president in charge of research, and Harold "Hal" Hamilton, founder and president of Winton, had perfected a two-cycle, eight-cylinder diesel engine that effectively doubled the horsepower per cylinder compared to a conventional four-cycle diesel. Hamilton had perfected an arrangement whereby a diesel engine generated electricity, which in turn powered a

An early drawing of the *Burlington Zephyr* was made in anticipation of the train's debut. The general lines of the first unit were followed in the final design, but note that the train is operated by one man—in uniform, no less. *RAILWAY AGE*

A later artist's conception of the *Burlington Zephyr* looked closer to the final product. The *Zephyr's* designer was an aeronautical engineer from the Massachusetts Institute of Technology, Albert Dean, who went to work for Budd shortly after graduation in 1931. His brother Walter Dean also worked for Budd as a mechanical engineer. *RAILWAY AGE*

traction motor located on locomotive axles. Diesel locomotives were not new.* As early as 1925 a diesel-electric-powered locomotive had been purchased by the Central Railroad of New Jersey. Within a span of eight years, numerous diesel-electric locomotives were working on America's railroads as switcher locomotives. Among their most salient attributes were their ability to work continuously with a minimum of servicing, but a diesel engine that would power a high-speed train was not yet in service.

Kettering's diesel had been refined with the use of new metal alloys that made the new engine lighter than previous models, about 21 pounds per horsepower (as opposed to 60 pounds for previous models) and powerful enough to pull a train. It could also be placed within a locomotive frame, setting the stage for a breakthrough in locomotive technology and a giant leap forward for the railroad industry.

What happened next was to have far-reaching significance in the annals of transportation. Ralph Budd was approached by Hal Hamilton who knew of Budd's order for a new train. Ralph Budd asked how long it would take to build such an engine. Although Hamilton's engine was not yet ready for production, he indicated that one might be ready within a month. Budd leapt at the opportunity, agreeing to place an order for the new diesel engine. Having had previous experience with diesel engines during his work on the Cascade Tunnel project, and having seen two experimental models at the GM exhibit at the Century of Progress Exhibition in Chicago, he recognized it would be much better suited for his train than the distillate type engine that had been used to power other experiments.

So it was that on June 17, 1933, the Burlington ordered a 600-hp Model 201A diesel engine from General Motors for the train then being assembled at the Edward G. Budd Manufacturing Company plant in Philadelphia.

With the train and power plant being built, the next issue was to determine where it would be placed in service. First, Budd and his staff decided that the new train had to be placed in operation where the railroad was presently losing money on existing service, yet where that service could not be discontinued because of

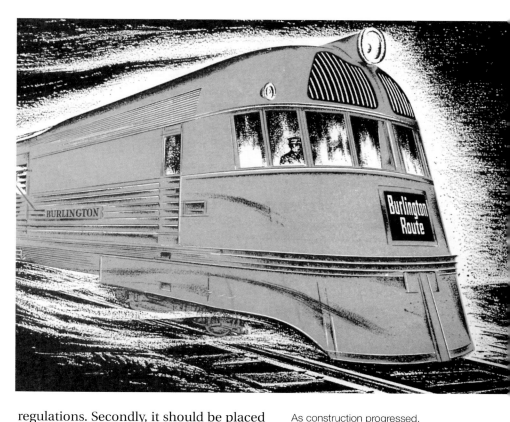

regulations. Secondly, it should be placed in a service where it could make at least one round trip each day and where servicing could be centralized. The run chosen was that between Kansas City and Lincoln, Nebraska.

With that much done, the third step was to decide on a name. The new train had to have a name, if only to maintain railroad tradition. A name would make the train special, and this train *was* special. Budd solicited suggestions from among his advisors.

Ralph Budd later described the occasion which produced the name *Zephyr*. It was during a meeting with his top associates that the subject came up. Albert Cotsworth, Jr., the railroad's general passenger traffic manager, "replied that nothing suitable had occurred to him yet, but that he had been meaning to look up the last word in the dictionary because without any question this would certainly be the 'last word' in passenger trains." Budd reached for the dictionary and soon began to laugh. The last word was "zymurgy," the practice or art of fermentation, as in wine-making, brewing, distilling, etc.

That wouldn't work. Cotsworth tried again, looking up the last word in another dictionary, turning up the work "zyzzle," to sputter, which was even worse. The

As construction progressed, advertising renderings more accurately reflected the *Zephyr's* final appearance. RAILWAY AGE

*Formed in 1922, EMC was the leading producer of diesel locomotives. Electro-Motive Company had marketed passenger railcars since 1924, with engines made by Winton. In 1930, General Motors bought Winton, then EMC, which became Electro-Motive Corporation. In 1941 EMC became a division of General Motors.

meeting concluded and Budd was left alone. Yet, Cotsworth's suggestion remained in Budd's mind and it prompted him to draw on his recall of some characters in Chaucer's classic, *Canterbury Tales*, a book he had been rereading. In it, the god of the west wind, Zephyrus, typified renaissance ("When April with its gentle showers has pierced the March drought to the root and bathed every plant in the moisture which will hasten the flowering; when Zephyrus with his sweet breath has stirred the new shoots in every wood and field, and the young sun has run its half-course in the Ram, and small birds sing melodiously, so touched in their hearts by Nature that they sleep all night with eyes open..."). That was it!

He went to the phone and called Cotsworth, telling him that he had a name to suggest which commenced with the last letter of the alphabet, even though it was not exactly the final word in the dictionary.

His suggestion: *Zephyr*.[6]

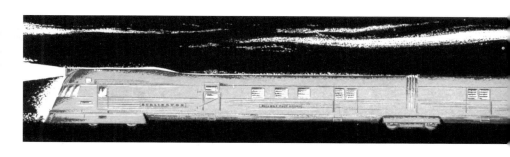

The *ZEPHYR* ... MADE POSSIBLE BY THE BUDD **SHOTWELD** SYSTEM OF STAINLESS ALL-STEEL CONSTRUCTION

Construction of the *Burlington Zephyr* at Budd's Philadelphia plant made use of less materials to effect a strong carbody, yet the overall materials costs were more expensive. This became an inhibiting factor to some railroads who remained loyal to Pullman-Standard. The durability of stainless steel was greater than the carbon steel then being used in railroad passenger car construction, which over time, became more expensive to maintain because of corrosion. This view reveals the intricate framework the company employed to build the *Zephyr*. BNSF ARCHIVES

A Budd employee works on top of one of the *Zephyr* carbodies in February 1934 with the Shotweld unit. This is the first carbody of the three-car train. Note the letterbox opening for the United States Post Office located in the center of the photograph. One could mail a letter in Lincoln in the early morning and have it delivered in Omaha or Kansas City for transmittal within a few hours. BOMBARDIER CORPORATION, MARK REUTTER COLLECTION

LEGENDS IN THEIR OWN TIME

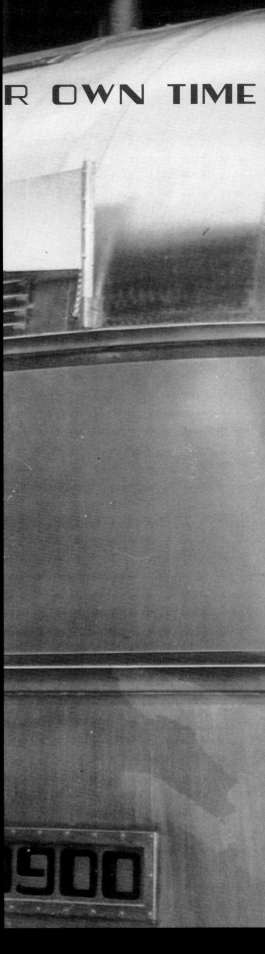

On April 7, 1934, the country's first streamlined diesel-powered train, the Burlington *Zephyr*, made its debut at the Edward G. Budd Manufacturing plant in Philadelphia. It was like nothing anyone had ever seen. The entire 72-seat train was only 197 feet in length, weighing approximately 100 tons, just slightly more than the weight of a single conventional railway car. With a fuel capacity of 600 gallons it was capable of traveling more than 1,000 miles before refueling was required—just enough for a full day's work. Because it was articulated, only 16 wheels were required to carry the train's weight, whereas a conventional train of three cars would have required 36 wheels.

No one was more qualified to have his picture taken in the engineer's seat in the new *Zephyr* than Ralph Budd, president of the Burlington Railroad, tipping his straw hat in greeting. The engineer's compartment had a window/vent which served as a unique air conditioning arrangement, which in this view appears to be in the open position. *BNSF ARCHIVES*

Two days later, on April 9, the train made the rail industry take notice that this was no ordinary experiment when it reached a speed of 104 mph on a trial run over the Pennsylvania Railroad between Philadelphia and Perkiomen Junction. What followed was a rapid-fire series of events. On April 17, the railroad accepted the new train and a christening ceremony was held the next afternoon at Philadelphia's Broad Street Station. Dignitaries in attendance were the two Budds, William Irvin, president of United States Steel, and Alfred Sloan, president of General Motors. The event was carried live over the NBC Radio Network. Unable to attend the ceremony was the president of the Pennsylvania Railroad, General William Atterbury, who spoke to the radio audience from the NBC studios at Radio City, congratulating Ralph Budd, saying whose "vision, courage, initiative and genuine railroad executive ability have made this new train possible." He also congratulated the officers and employees of the many manufacturing organizations whose products had been used in the train's construction. Gerard Swope of General Electric, also in New York speaking over the radio, spoke about the extent that electricity played a role in the Shotweld process and in the ways the train had become a success.

Edward Budd paid tribute to those who had been instrumental in producing the train, and noted that Ralph Budd had shown an interest in the new type of equipment since the Budd Company had built its first rail car in 1932. Alfred Sloan, president of General Motors, remarked upon the amount of scientific research that had gone into the *Zephyr*, while William Irvin of United States Steel spoke about the development of stainless steel.

After the first round of speeches, there was a vicarious tour of the train, by way of description for the radio audience and broadcast over speakers for the assembled guests, conducted by Owen Cunningham of Philadelphia's WLIT Radio. While comfortably nestled in one of the stuffed chairs in the train's observation lounge, he gave those listening his impressions of the various features of the train.

Ralph Budd spoke and thanked all those who had made the train possible and then announced when and where the new train would be operated. The honor of smashing a bottle of champagne to christen the train fell to Marguerite Cotsworth, a student at Swarthmore College and the daughter of Albert Cotsworth, Jr. When the bottle broke, a cacophony of sirens, bells and whistles from locomotives in the terminal filled the air.

Following the ceremonies, and after which more than 24,000 visitors went through it, the train embarked on an extensive three-week exhibition tour of 30 eastern cities, including Wilmington, Delaware, Washington, D.C., Trenton, New Brunswick, and Newark, New Jersey; both Pennsylvania Station and Grand Central Station in New York; Bridgeport and New Haven, Connecticut; Providence, Rhode Island; Boston, Worcester, and Springfield, Massachusetts; Albany, Schenectady, Utica, Syracuse, Rochester, and Buffalo, New York; Detroit, Michigan; Toledo, Cleveland, Columbus, and Cincinnati, Ohio; Pittsburgh, Pennsylvania; Louisville, Kentucky; and Indianapolis

text continued on page 30

In an early construction photo of the *Burlington Zephyr* taken at the Edward G. Budd Manufacturing Company in Philadelphia on March 16, 1934, we can see how the smooth sheets of stainless steel have been applied to the framework and how craftsmen have left a clear space where the BURLINGTON ROUTE shield will be placed on the locomotive's nose. This contour will soon become the railroad's ambassador in a nationwide tour. *BOMBARDIER CORPORATION, MARK REUTTER COLLECTION*

Floor plan of the three-car *Burlington Zephyr* as delivered. KEVIN J. HOLLAND COLLECTION

right: Front view of the *Zephyr*. RAILWAY AGE

far right: This overhead view of the engine room, looking forward, shows the radiator fans and the 600-hp Winton diesel engine. RAILWAY AGE

bottom: The interior of the *Zephyr* cab is viewed while the train is still at Budd's plant in Philadelphia. The cab had a single seat—for the engineer, or "motorman," as he was called—positioned almost center. A position for a fireman was not envisioned as the train was equipped with a "deadman's pedal," seen on the floor directly in front of the seat. As long as the engineer kept the pedal depressed with his foot—ten pounds of pressure was required—the automatic brake would not activate. It was a safety device that the designers and the railroad believed obviated the necessity of a second crew person. The design of the front gave the engineer an almost complete 180-degree view, but there was little to protect the crew from obstructions in the train's path, as the Burlington would tragically find out. BNSF ARCHIVES

far left: The main passenger compartment of the *Zephyr*, with its large plate glass windows, was bright and unencumbered by luggage racks. *RAILWAY AGE*

left: The rounded rear end of the *Zephyr* was without a tail sign. In later versions, this oversight would be addressed. Picture windows afforded passengers a panoramic view. *RAILWAY AGE*

below: In this slightly retouched view of the solarium lounge, the Budd Company has created an inviting environment. For 1934, this was a novel form of luxury travel. *BNSF ARCHIVES*

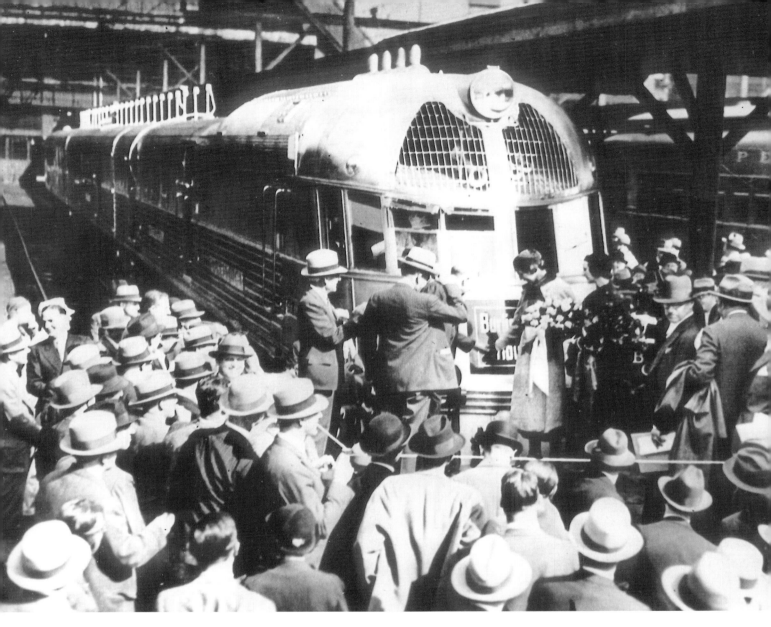

text continued on page 34

On April 17, 1934, the Burlington Railroad staged a christening ceremony at Philadelphia's Broad Street Station. Dignitaries from United States Steel and General Motors were present along with Ralph and Edward Budd. The event was broadcast live over the NBC Radio Network. In this view, we see Edward Budd speaking with Marguerite Cotsworth, daughter of Albert Cotsworth, Jr., the railroad's general passenger agent, perhaps instructing her as to where the bottle of champagne should be broken. The christening ceremony at Broad Street Station was only the first of many events to follow, heralding the arrival of the new train and the dawn of a new era in American railroading. *BNSF ARCHIVES*

and Fort Wayne, Indiana. During this whirlwind exercise, approximately 380,000 visitors inspected the *Zephyr*. On May 11 it arrived in Chicago, where in two days close to 34,000 visitors toured the train, and after its two-day exhibition in Chicago, it left for a two-week tour where it stopped in 16 cities along the Burlington Route.

The train was "headline news," and the next step was to keep the publicity machine at a fever pitch. But, how to do it? Whether it was Budd's idea or one that germinated through a discussion is not clear, but certainly all were in agreement that the railroad should capitalize on the publicity already generated by the train and stage some stunt that would further capture the public's attention. An inauguration ceremony had already been held,

so something that could effectively produce fireworks by way of demonstrating the train's revolutionary capabilities was what the railroad really needed. A non-stop long-distance run would fit the criteria—and that's exactly what Budd championed: a non-stop 1000-mile run between Denver and Chicago. He suggested that the train should leave Denver in the morning and arrive in Chicago that very evening. To make it even more exciting, the train could by-pass Union Station and instead roll to a stop on the center stage of the current exposition, "A Century of Progress," then being held on the shores of Lake Michigan. Budd felt the event could be carefully arranged with exposition officials and timed so that arrival would occur just at the moment of

On April 22, 1934, the *Burlington Zephyr* No. 9900 was on tour, traveling to New York's Pennsylvania Station from Washington, D. C., where it had been put on display. The train is seen on the electrified Pennsylvania Railroad tracks west of Trenton, New Jersey. *W. R. OSBORNE, TLC COLLECTION*

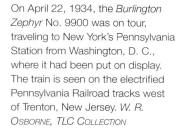

The *Zephyr* made many appearances in the Northeast before being sent to Chicago for display and the start of a nationwide tour. Here the train is at Washington Union Station in April 1934. The *Zephyrs* were numbered in the 9900 series as the Burlington had begun numbering its internal-combustion locomotives starting at No. 9000. The next open series was 9900, following the coach/baggage/mail motor cars in the 9800 series. *TLC COLLECTION*

In another view taken at Washington, D.C., the train serves as a backdrop for those who want to be photographed with the latest symbol of modern train design. *TLC COLLECTION*

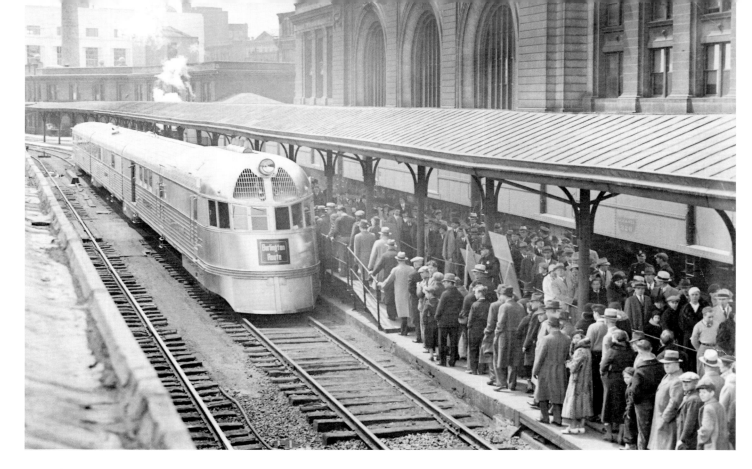

above: The *Zephyr* made a tour of eastern cities including stops along the New York Central Railroad and its subsidiaries. On April 28, 1934, the 9900 is on display at Albany (N.Y.) Union Station. *JACK MOWER, COURTESY OF KALMBACH PUBLISHING COMPANY, TRAINS MAGAZINE COLLECTION*

middle: In late May, the *Zephyr* was sent to Denver in preparation for a dawn-to-dusk non-stop run of over 1,000 miles. Days before, the train was placed on display in the rail yard in Denver. The entire 72-seat train was 197 feet in length, weighing approximately 100 tons. *L. C. MCCLURE*

bottom: The middle car contained a baggage/express compartment, a small kitchenette/buffet and a small coach section. Note the streamlined decorated truck housing covers, designed to reduce wind resistance in concert with the underbody skirting. This view also shows the unique diaphragm arrangement between the train's three sections. Passenger access was through the vertically split doors. *OTTO PERRY, DENVER PUBLIC LIBRARY WESTERN HISTORY DEPARTMENT*

The locomotive contained an operator's compartment, behind which was located a 600-hp Model 201A diesel engine made by Winton, a division of General Motors. The *Zephyr* was supported by 16 wheels, as compared with a conventional train of three cars which would have required 36 wheels. OTTO PERRY, DENVER PUBLIC LIBRARY WESTERN HISTORY DEPARTMENT

The observation car carried the train's number rather than a car number. Nothing like this train had ever been seen before and what attention it generated! These photographs, taken on May 23, 1934, were made just three days before its historic run. Many adventures lay before it. OTTO PERRY, DENVER PUBLIC LIBRARY WESTERN HISTORY DEPARTMENT

The observation car's solarium lounge design was marred only by the boxy marker lights and the backup light located above the windows. Still, these were matters of necessity rather than of aesthetics. Years later, the practice would be repeated on the railroad's observation cars built for the *California Zephyr*. OTTO PERRY, DENVER PUBLIC LIBRARY WESTERN HISTORY DEPARTMENT

the grand climax of railroad publicist Edward Hungerford's pageant, "Wings of a Century."

This daring and unprecedented non-stop run would take 14 hours, cutting 12 hours from the current Denver–Chicago run. With no time to lose, the historic trip was planned for May 26, 1934, and to make certain that the run would happen without mishap, the railroad planned the trip down to the smallest detail, including the guarding of all rail/highway grade crossings. Timing was of the utmost importance, with little room allowed for mistakes or emergencies. Everything had to work precisely ... or else.

That "or else" came dangerously close. In 1960, Harry C. Murphy recounted how twelve hours before the early morning departure, railroad technicians discovered a broken armature bearing in one of the lead traction motors. As soon as Ralph Budd was told of the problem,

he and his advisors furtively began looking for solutions.

Here was the Burlington Railroad, poised to make history. The line between Denver and Chicago had been inspected and in places adjusted to carry the high-speed train. The company's publicists had a golden opportunity to create headlines that would keep the railroad in the fore-front of favorable public opinion—dozens of newspapers had sent reporters and photographers to Denver to record the event. Platoons of people were ready to keep the public off the tracks and at grade crossings. Approximately $50,000 had been spent just for safety arrangements alone, and countless thousands of men, women and children would be lining the tracks to watch the passing train.

There wasn't much hope of finding a replacement, though. EMC's representative said the nearest part was in Detroit, but could be flown to Denver within a few days' time. That wasn't good enough. Somebody remarked that the rival Union Pacific would be pretty happy to see the new *Zephyr* stalled by a broken part—and that gave Ralph Budd an idea.

He picked up the telephone and made a frantic call to an acquaintance of his, Carl Gray, president of the Union Pacific Railroad. The Union Pacific had its own (similar) train that used bearings of the same type. Maybe, Budd thought, the UP could be persuaded to loan the Burlington a spare.

At his home, Gray assured Budd that the bearing would be made available, but it was in Omaha, not Denver! Gray told Budd, however, that he would immediately arrange to have one of his mechanical people board a plane at Omaha with the part and fly it to Cheyenne, and from there, a chartered plane could fly him to Denver. Upon landing at Denver, Fred Gurley, Burlington's assistant vice president, met the plane and he and the bearing received a police escort to the Burlington shops.

The Burlington's publicity representative opined that the Union Pacific would have a field day with the story of how it saved the Burlington's new train on its initial run. Ralph Budd suggested that the Burlington should be gracious enough to tell the story, much to the horror of those assembled. The Union Pacific, Budd reminded everyone present, was not

Seen shortly after its sunrise departure from Denver, the *Zephyr* races east near Keenesburg, Colorado, at an estimated 85 mph. It appears that the crowd in the cab is undaunted by the lack of seats as they have the best view of what lies ahead. *OTTO PERRY, DENVER PUBLIC LIBRARY WESTERN HISTORY DEPARTMENT*

viewing the event as a rivalry, but one of historic importance— the story should be told and those deserving credit should have their day.

With the scheduled departure from Denver set for 4:00 a.m., that deadline was going to be missed, maybe by as much as an hour. The Burlington's mechanical forces set to work and the bearing was hurriedly installed overnight. It was not an auspicious start.

At exactly 5:05 a.m. on May 26, the three-car *Zephyr*, consisting of a power car (which also had space for a railway post office), a baggage-express/buffet-passenger car and coach-observation-

Later in the day, the *Zephyr* is seen passing a crowd as it descends the hill into Burlington, Iowa. Crowds formed all along the route of the train between Denver and Chicago as it sped by. Some schools closed and all the grade crossings and "interlocking" railroad junctions were guarded so nothing would slow the train's progress as it raced into the history books. *COURTESY KALMBACH PUBLISHING COMPANY, TRAINS MAGAZINE COLLECTION*

After averaging a speed of 77.6 mph, the *Zephyr* arrived at the Chicago lakefront at exactly 8:09 p.m. on the stage of Edward Hungerford's "Wings of a Century" at the Century of Progress Exposition. The train had averaged 2.77 miles per gallon of fuel during the trip at a cost of only $14.64. During the trip it had attained a top speed of 112.5 mph. *BNSF ARCHIVES*

*The editor of Denver's *Rocky Mountain News* presented a donkey to the Century of Progress Exposition, and had arranged to send it east on the special run of the new train. "When shall I bring it over?" asked the editor on the telephone. Edward Flynn, the railroad's vice president of operations, turned to Ralph Budd in astonishment upon learning of this new wrinkle while the *Zephyr* was still being repaired, and asked how he should respond. Budd reputedly replied, "Why not? One more jackass on this trip won't make any difference!" The railroad brought in some hay and tied up the burro, now named "Zeph," in the baggage compartment.

lounge car, complete with officials and an unlikely guest, a burro mascot, departed Denver Union Station heading east—a green flag borrowed from the Indianapolis Speedway being used to initiate the ceremonial start. The population of small towns, notified in advance of the historic trip, came out by the hundreds to watch the train flash through their towns.*

As the train was well underway, and it seemed as though nothing could mar the festive mood of those inside, near panic erupted when someone accidentally shut a steel door on an electric cable that short-circuited the starting mechanism. Instinctively, Ernie Kuehn, the train's Winton Company engineer, shut off the engine, but with a damaged cable it could not be restarted. The train, now coasting down a 45-mile descent, was slowly losing momentum as another frantic search was made, this time for a splice, so that the train could maintain its "non-stop" run performance. All the while, the train was slowing to its minimum speed of 15 mph before the straight-air service brakes would be applied automatically. As Ralph Budd later explained to a meeting of the Chicago Traffic Club, "Roy Baer, an engineer from Electro-Motive, held a bare end of the cable in each hand. He jammed the two ends together and a brilliant spark leaped across the gap which burned Baer's hands. The engine roared into life."[7] At 18 mph, the *Zephyr* was rolling under its own power again.

Then, at West Burlington, technicians noticed a serious drop in air pressure. This was due to a heavy air brake application and many whistle blows for grade crossings while traveling through Burlington. The engineer, now a Burlington employee, had to suspend whistle use and utilized the bell instead so that the air compressor could build back pressure. The low air pressure was about to trigger an automatic and unwanted service brake application, again threatening the non-stop performance.[8] At the critical moment, Ernie Kuehn stepped forward and pulled the throttle wide open, momentarily setting the air compressor into activity and filling the air reservoir. They were back in business.

With all 1,689 highway grade crossings between Denver and Chicago guarded by an estimated 3,500 local police and railroad officials, and between 700 and 900 volunteer guards (Scouts, Kiwanis, Rotary, local citizens, etc.), and all switches between Denver and Chicago lined and spiked, and clear track ahead assured by the operating department (all trains in advance of the *Zephyr's* approach were stopped), the train headed east. At exactly 8:09 p.m., the *Zephyr* arrived on the stage of Hungerford's "Wings of a Century," and the crowd went crazy. Sensing how to pull off an encore, Ralph Budd himself led Zeph out of his compartment and presented the mascot to the exposition's officials.

As if the trip wasn't impressive enough, exceeding Ralph Budd's most optimistic expectations, the train had averaged 2.77 miles per gallon of fuel during the trip. At the cost of four cents a gallon, the trip had cost exactly $14.64. In addition, the *Zephyr* had attained a top speed of 112.5 mph between Yuma and Wray, Colorado. The train had traveled 1,015.4 miles at an average speed of 77.61 mph, making up the lost hour at Denver. There was no doubt—a new age was born for American railroading.

Following a brief period where the train was on display at the fair, the *Zephyr* embarked on a tour westward where it took part in the opening of the new Dotsero Cutoff, west of the Moffat Tunnel, in a ceremony at Bond, Colorado. After a tour of the West Coast, it returned to Chicago in mid-July via the Royal Gorge.

Back in the Windy City again, the *Zephyr* was placed on display for two weeks at the World's Fairgrounds in

Stainless steel matchbook covers were created as mementos of the run. *Kevin J. Holland Collection*

Ralph Budd poses along with Fred Gurley (later president of the Santa Fe), seated first at left, and Albert Cotsworth, seated right rear. *BNSF Archives*

The day after the *Zephyr's* non-stop run, the train was placed on display at the 1934 World's Fair in Chicago. Visitors line up to see the country's newest train. *BNSF Archives*

In a view from August 1, 1934, the crowds have thinned somewhat at the World's Fair in Chicago, but the *Zephyr* is still the center of attention. Soon it will be embarking on another tour. *Otto Perry, Denver Public Library Western History Department*

Albert Cotsworth, Jr., holds the reins to "Zeph," the *Zephyr* mascot, with members of the "Dawn-to-Dusk Club." Next to Cotsworth are representatives from Winton Engine Corporation, the General Electric Company, Westinghouse Air Brake Company, and others. A total of 36 officers of the Burlington Railroad rode the train in addition to 20 newspaper reporters, along with Edward G. Budd, president of the Budd Company, and Ralph Budd, president of the Burlington. *H. M. Rhoades, Denver Public Library Western History Department*

Chicago where close to 709,000 visitors went through the train.

Now, it was time to get down to business. At the end of the month it was removed from the fair long enough to be placed on a run between Chicago and the Twin Cities (on July 30) to see what sort of schedule could be established. It made the run in six hours flat, averaging a speed of 71 mph.

Despite the need to get the train into service, still more testing had to be performed and it had to fulfill more public relations and marketing functions. On August 1 it was returned to the fair and after the Labor Day weekend, the *Zephyr* was sent west where it took the pivotal role in RKO's production of "The Silver Streak." The movie—and the train—was an instant hit at the box office with Depression-era audiences.

Between November 3 and November 10, the railroad operated a number of excursions on the train in order to satisfy the curiosity of the public along the line and thus reduce the number of persons who would try to ride the train on its inaugural run. Round-trip excursions were operated out of Lincoln, Omaha, Council Bluffs, St. Joseph, Weston, Atchison, Leavenworth, and Kansas City. Even on a rainy November 3 at Lincoln, 217 persons paid a dollar each to be carried on seven trips of one hour's duration. At Omaha on November 4, a total of 434 persons (at $1.25 each) were carried on seven trips of ninety minutes each. At Council Bluffs on November 5, a further 342 persons were carried—at 75 cents each—on five trips of about one hour's duration.

The demand for space on the three-car train was such that reservations were closed several days in advance when requests amounted to several hundred. In order to provide for holders of through tickets, the sale of local tickets between Omaha and Lincoln was limited to fifty.

With trials and exhibition runs over for the moment, the *Zephyr* became the first diesel-electric streamlined train to enter regular railway service on November 11, 1934, as trains Nos. 20 and 21. Its schedule called for leaving Lincoln, Nebraska, in the early morning where it traveled through Omaha to Kansas City, returning that evening, maximizing utilization. The entire round trip would cover 500 miles in one day. Patronage on the train continued to be heavy on November 12, the second day of the scheduled operation. On the southbound trip, 36 passengers embarked at Lincoln while another 43 boarded at Council Bluffs. The maximum number on the train at any time was 50, with 47 persons transported into Kansas City.

Besides the demonstrated virtues of the train's design and performance, there were its innovative amenities, one of which was how it delivered meals on board. Burlington dining car services were usually a money-losing operation, so they were seeking low-cost alternatives to this otherwise expensive-to-deliver service. The solution appeared to be serving meals at the passenger's seat on fold-out trays and tables. Meals were served and delivered from a compact buffet-grill located in the middle car of the train, and this became one of the focal points of the railroad's advertising and that of the Budd Company.

Suppliers of materials used in the train, such as manufacturers of safety

appliances, seats, and other equipment, were quick to latch onto the popularity of the new train, highlighting the use of their products on the *Zephyr*. It seems that everyone wanted to "get on board" and share in the train's success.

The first week of operation was not without its incidents, however. On November 13, a farmer's truck ran into the side of the train as it headed westbound passing through Greenwood, Nebraska, 17 miles east of Lincoln, traveling at about 34 mph. No one was injured in the incident and the damage to the train consisted of a broken step on the first car and a dent in the body. The truck ran into the mail section of the first car and the impact swung the truck so that its rear end

On June 16, 1934, the *Zephyr* was sent west for the official opening of the Denver & Rio Grande Western's "Dotsero Cut-off" where it is seen leaving Denver. The cut-off provided a new and shorter transcontinental route by way of Orestod, Colorado. *Otto Perry, Denver Public Library Western History Department*

The *Zephyr* is seen traveling through Colorado on the tracks of the Denver & Rio Grande Western. After another appearance at the World's Fair, the train was sent west to take part in the filming of "Silver Streak," RKO's epic adventure movie. *Electro-Motive, Kevin J. Holland Collection*

scratched and dented the body of that car. The *Zephyr* was delayed only fifteen minutes at Lincoln.

By the end of the week, 35 percent more passengers rode the train (during the week of November 12-18) than had ridden the steam-powered train in the preceding week. The average patronage between all points was 91 persons as compared with 67 on the former train.

A questionnaire given to passengers returned figures showing that 18 percent traveled from curiosity; 67 percent would have used Burlington steam train service regardless, ten percent would have used some other steam train, and five percent would have gone by private automobile, bus, or airplane. The distance traveled per passenger on the *Zephyr* increased sharply with 44 persons being carried per train-mile as compared with 21 persons per train-mile the week before.

On two trips, southbound on November 17, and northbound on November 18 (Saturday and Sunday, respectively), the *Zephyr's* 72-passenger seating capacity proved inadequate. On the Sunday run out of Kansas City there were 90 passengers, including 41 curiosity riders.[9]

The train's schedule was maintained each day, except for the fifteen minute delay westbound at Greenwood on November 13. Comparing business on the train for the week of November 12-18 as contrasted with steam trains on the corresponding schedule during the week of November 4-10, there was an increase of

96 percent in passengers traveling between Lincoln and Omaha. Southbound, leaving Omaha and Council Bluffs, passengers for all points averaged 42 per trip as compared with 18 the previous week, an increase of 133 percent. Southbound into Kansas City, passengers from all points averaged 53 per trip as compared with 29 the previous week, an increase of 83 percent.

Northbound out of Kansas City, passengers for all points averaged 57 per trip as compared with 25 the previous week, an increase of 128 percent. Northbound into Council Bluffs and Omaha, passengers from all points averaged 44 per trip as compared with 17 the previous week, an increase of 160 percent.

Gross revenue per train-mile was $1.65, of which about $1.00 was from passenger receipts, compared with passenger revenue of about 50 cents per train-mile on the steam trains.

The results for the Burlington were astounding. Passenger miles on the Burlington as a whole for December 1934 and January 1935 increased 26 percent over the same two-month period of the previous year. Mileage traveled by patrons on the *Zephyr* increased 193 percent over the same two months of the previous year on the trains that the *Zephyr* had replaced. Curiously, as a by-product, two remaining steam-powered trains operating between Omaha and Kansas City experienced the same increase compared to the system as a whole.

opposite: In addition to appearing in the movie, the *Zephyr* went on a tour of West Coast cities before returning to the Midwest where it operated in excursion service prior to its inaugural revenue run. In this view, the train is dwarfed by the Royal Gorge while on the Rio Grande. *Electro-Motive, Kevin J. Holland Collection*

above: Two eras of railroad transportation met while the *Zephyr* traveled through Colorado on its western tour. *TLC Collection*

Demand for space on the new train was so great that the railroad ordered an additional coach car to be added to the trainset. This September 27, 1935, view at Omaha shows the train as it would appear for much of the next 25 years of its service life. *OTTO PERRY, DENVER PUBLIC LIBRARY WESTERN HISTORY DEPARTMENT*

In another view of the *Zephyr*, now called the *Pioneer Zephyr*, the train is traveling 20 mph as train No. 20, photographed near Council Bluffs, Iowa, on May 29, 1938. The downward scowl of the locomotive vents above the operator's cab was a design not repeated in subsequent *Zephyr* orders, but the grill motif and the windows underneath with the railroad herald would be replicated in diesel locomotive orders that would follow in the form of E5s, E7s, and E9s. *OTTO PERRY, DENVER PUBLIC LIBRARY WESTERN HISTORY DEPARTMENT*

By the end of the first year of the train's operation, it had operated 177,000 revenue miles of service, running daily, with only eleven days being out of service for required maintenance. Although the initial cost of the *Zephyr* was close to double that of an equivalent steam-powered train, the lower cost of operation made up for the difference. The *Burlington Zephyr* had proven its value. A year-end evaluation revealed that it had carried an average of 204 passengers per day for an average distance of 114 miles. This represented an increase of 50 percent in the number of passengers carried compared with the steam-powered trains that were replaced. It was also an increase of 113 percent in passenger miles. Operating and maintenance costs of the *Zephyr* during its first year in operation averaged 35 cents per train-mile, as compared with 59 cents for the steam-powered trains. Although the train was more expensive to purchase, the savings from the vantage of

fuel costs, reduced maintenance, and higher equipment utilization, allowed the Burlington to pay for the *Zephyr* in only 20 months.

Obviously, the railroad had a winner. The one drawback to the *Zephyr*, though, was its limited capacity, so in an attempt to rectify this problem, the railroad ordered a fourth chair car to be added to the three-car train, which was done in June 1935.

With such a new high-speed train in service, it didn't take long for other railroads in competition with the Burlington to recognize that they had to act fast if they were to compete effectively. In the case of the Missouri Pacific, it cut the running times of its Omaha-Kansas City steam trains Nos. 105 and 106 to three hours and fifty-nine minutes for the 199-mile run. The Burlington, not to be outdone, quickened the schedule of its *Zephyr* to reduce its four-hour run to three hours and fifty-five minutes for the 196 miles between those two points.

The Missouri Pacific train, now known as *The Marathon*, left Omaha at 8:00 a.m. instead of 8:05 and arrived at Kansas City at 11:59 a.m. instead of 1:30, with an average speed of 49.96 mph. The returning train left Kansas City at 4:30 p.m. instead of 4:10 p.m., and arrived in Omaha at 8:29 p.m. instead of 9:15 p.m. The Missouri Pacific train consisted of a standard baggage car, air-conditioned deluxe coaches, and an air-conditioned dining-parlor car, with air-conditioned coaches between Lincoln and Union.[10]

Even before the *Zephyr* had been placed in regular service in July 1934, the board of directors of the Chicago, Burlington & Quincy placed an order with the Budd Manufacturing Company for the construction of two additional high-speed streamlined three-car articulated trains, similar to the *Zephyr*. These two trains would be placed in regular daylight service between Chicago and Minneapolis-St. Paul, Minnesota, between which points they would operate in opposite directions on a daily basis.

Unlike the first *Zephyr*, however, the new trains would not contain a mail compartment, with the additional space being used for baggage, express, and additional passenger seating. With a few extra modifications, these two new *Zephyrs* would be identical twins.

MAKING HISTORY—
BY THE BOOK

As the *Zephyr* was a new form of technology, the railroad was not completely prepared to have members of its engineer's roster step into the cab of the locomotive and begin work. This didn't mean that the railroad was exempt from existing labor agreements, however. Even though nothing like the train had been envisioned by the unions or management before, the terms of agreements still in force required standard considerations.

One agreement stipulated that should a special train be dispatched, the locomotive could be operated by a division road foreman who would not be subject to the infamous "100-mile rule," but that the displaced engineer(s) from the brotherhood would still receive a day's pay for "time not worked." In the case of the *Zephyr*, Winton's chief mechanical engineer, Ernie Kuehn, was at the throttle of the train most of the time during the exhibition tours, assisted by a qualified railroad pilot who would call signals and announce speed restrictions and other requirements of the road. When the train operated between Denver and Chicago on May 26, Ernie Kuehn was again at the throttle as it departed Denver, but as the trip would be a day-long affair, replacements in the form of division road foremen and mechanical engineers, were on hand to take over during the journey.

Crew members on that historic trip included:
Jack Ford, CB&Q Assistant Master Mechanic (engineer)
Ernie Weber, CB&Q Sup't of Automated Equipment (engineer)
Ernie Kuehn, Winton Engine Company (engineer)
H. R. Clark, CB&Q pilot
Harry C. Murphy, CB&Q pilot (later president of CB&Q)
E. H. Piper, CB&Q pilot
W. O. Frame, CB&Q pilot
W. H. Dungan, CB&Q Road Foreman
O. E. Hoenshell, CB&Q Road Foreman
W. A. Strauss, CB&Q Road Foreman
E. Milar, CB&Q Road Foreman
Raymond Wells, CB&Q Conductor
Ed J. Ross, CB&Q Dining Car Inspector
Wayne Wigton, CB&Q Signal Department (radioman)

The list of railroad officials included, in part, Ralph Budd, president; Edward Flynn, vice president; H. H. Holcomb, vice president; Robert Rice, vice president; T. J. Thomas, assistant to the president; Fred G. Gurley, assistant to vice president; W. E. Fuller, assistant to vice president; Albert Cotsworth, passenger traffic manager; A. W. Newton, engineer; H. H. Urbach, superintendent motor power; Frank Darrow, chief engineer; Neil Olsen, special agent; J. H. Aydelott, general manager Western Lines, W. F. Thiehoff, general manager Eastern Lines; and E. C. Anderson, mechanical engineer.

Passengers included, in part, Walter Anderson, son of E. C. Anderson; Thomas M. Henkle; Harold Hamilton, Winton Engine Company; Roy Baer, assistant chief engineer, Electro-Motive Corporation; Edward G. Budd; Hal Foust, correspondent *Chicago Tribune*; Garet Garet, correspondent *Saturday Evening Post*; Alan C. McIntosh, correspondent *Lincoln Evening-Journal Star*; Joseph McMeel, correspondent *Rocky Mountain News*.

In addition, there were other correspondents of the media on board, and, of course, the burro mascot. The train had a seating capacity for 72 passengers, but because of the intense interest, ten additional chairs were set up in the baggage section for the overflow. These people had the additional honor of riding with "Zeph."

Suppliers of *Zephyr* components were eager to bask in the new streamliner's glow and promote their contributions. *TLC COLLECTION*

THE TWIN ZEPHYRS

In many respects, *Twin Zephyrs* Nos. 9901 and 9902 were identical in design to the original *Zephyr*. They differed in that they did not contain an RPO section and the operator's compartment windows did not sport the downward feature, or scowl, of the original train. The first car was also seven feet shorter than the original due to the elimination of the PRO space—although the unit contained a Railway Express Agency compartment for baggage and express. The *Twins* posed at Chicago Union Station on April 16, 1935, shortly after delivery. *CB&Q, KEVIN J. HOLLAND COLLECTION*

Attempting to duplicate the success of the *Burlington Zephyr*, the company hoped to remain in the forefront of the new diesel revolution by inaugurating its new *Twin Zephyrs*. The first of the two new trains arrived in early April 1935. The pair was an instant success with the public.

Capitalizing on the great popularity of the original *Zephyr*, the inauguration of the *Twin Zephyrs* was preceded by several events designed to attract widespread attention. On March 23, 1935, one of the *Twin Zephyrs*, No. 9901, carried 88 passengers for a trip over the Seaboard Air Line Railroad to points in Florida, visiting Washington, Fredericksburg, Richmond, Raleigh, Columbia, Savannah, Jacksonville, Ocala, Winter Haven, Sebring, West Palm Beach, Miami, Tampa, St. Petersburg, and Sarasota.

The trip was completed on April 2, by which time a total of 136,237 persons had inspected it. During the course of this

No. 9901 is departing West Trenton, N.J., on the Reading Railroad for a test run to Philadelphia. The date is March 16, 1935, and this is the *Twin Zephyr's* first trip out. *TLC COLLECTION*

journey of 2,861 miles, only $43.72 worth of fuel was consumed.

On April 6, the same trainset covered the 431 miles between Chicago and St. Paul in 5 hours and 33 minutes at an average speed of 77.7 mph. The occasion was a trial run with railway officers on board to test the train and track prior to the inauguration of regular service. At one time during the run, the train reached a speed of 104 mph. Leaving Chicago at 8:10 a.m., it arrived at St. Paul at 1:43 p.m.

The train had an enlarged fuel capacity from that of No. 9900. With a tank capacity of 660 gallons, fuel performance was 2.6 miles per gallon of fuel oil burned, with lubricating oil consumption restricted to two gallons for the entire round trip.

Following this trial run, the train departed for St. Louis, where on April 8 and 9, it carried members of the St. Louis Chamber of Commerce on a two-day trip with stops at Galesburg, Illinois, and at Burlington, Iowa. The following day, No. 9901 departed from Kansas City on a three-day trip carrying members of the Kansas City Chamber of Commerce, visiting Lincoln and McCook, Nebraska. At midnight on April 13, it departed Kansas City for Aurora (just west of Chicago) where it arrived at noon on April 14 to be united with its twin. This trainset, No. 9902, which had left Philadelphia on April 9, arrived in Chicago on April 11. On April 13, it traveled to Aurora for a ceremony which once again had been devised to garner maximum attention.

What would the railroad's publicity bureau conjure up for this occasion? Always prepared for an encore, 44 sets of twins had been selected by the railroad to participate in the celebration at Aurora. These human duplicates came from towns along the Burlington's route and had been ferried to Aurora for this unique occasion. Ranging in ages from 3 to 73 years, one of each pair of the twins was assigned to each of the trains. Following the festivities, the two trains traveled abreast of each other on the three-track main line from Aurora to Chicago, in yet another public relations stroke of genius.

The actual christening ceremony of the *Twin Zephyrs* took place at Chicago Union Station the next day—April 15—when 13-year-old twin sisters Marion and Frances Beeler simultaneously broke a bottle of champagne on each train. Fol-

lowing this august occasion, the trains began their non-stop journey to the Twin Cities carrying 120 members of the Chicago Association of Commerce. Both trains left Chicago Union Station at 7:30 a.m., one arriving in St. Paul at 1:15 p.m. and the other at 1:36 p.m.

In St. Paul, a special luncheon was held at the Minnesota Club, after which the guests boarded buses for the short trip to Minneapolis, where they then re-boarded the trains at 4:00 p.m. for the return trip to Chicago, one arriving at 10:09 p.m., and the other shortly thereafter.

On April 16, both trains were exhibited at Union Station and on the following day they were placed in service carrying excursionists between Chicago and Aurora.

On April 18, both trains were exhibited at the Great Northern station in Minneapolis, and on the 19th, at Union Station in St. Paul. On April 20, *Twin Zephyr* No. 9902 returned to Chicago and on April 21, both trains began their daily scheduled runs in regular service.

It was quite a common practice to be photographed with the new train. At extreme left in this view is Henry Anderson, a receiver of the Seaboard Air Line Railroad. Next to him is Edward G. Budd, president of the Budd Company; two unidentified individuals; and at extreme right, Norman Call, president of the Richmond, Fredericksburg & Potomac. The date is March 23, 1935, at Broad Street Station in Richmond, Virginia. While it was on exhibit at Broad Street Station, the *Twin Zephyr* was seen by 12,645 visitors, one of whom appears to be sneaking a peek inside the engineer's compartment. *WILLIAM E. GRIFFIN, JR. COLLECTION*

In another view taken at Broad Street Station in Richmond, Virginia, the Burlington's Road Foreman of Engines, Jack Ford, shakes hands with one of the officials present at the ceremony. Edward Budd is second from left. The train was operated by motormen from the Winton Company, with the railroads providing pilots and train crews. *WILLIAM E. GRIFFIN, JR. COLLECTION*

Memorandum for file: "Burlington Zephyr." *WILLIAM E. GRIFFIN, JR. COLLECTION*

FLORIDA TRIP OF BURLINGTON ZEPHYR #9901

At conference in Richmond, Wednesday, March 6th, at which were present representatives of the RF&P, S.A.L., Burlington, Budd and Winton Companies, the following arrangements were outlined for this trip, all subject to such modifications as developments may require:

1 - ITINERARY - SOUTHBOUND:

Lv. Washington	RF&P	10:00 A.M.	Sat. March 23rd
Stop Fredericksburg		About 11:00 A.M.	
Ar. Richmond		12:00 Noon	
Private Exhibition - Broad St. Station		1:00 PM to 1:30 PM	
Public		1:30 PM to 9:00 PM	
		8:00 A.M.	Sun. March 24th
Lv. Richmond	SAL	11:45 A.M.	
Ar. Raleigh		11:45 A.M. to 1:45 P.M.	
Public Exhibition - Union Station			
		1:45 P.M.	Sun. March 24th
Lv. Raleigh	SAL	6:15 P.M.	
Ar. Columbia			
Public Exhibition Seaboard Passenger Station, 6:15 PM to 8:15 PM			
		8:15 P.M.	Sun. March 24th
Lv. Columbia	SAL	11:30 P.M.	
Ar. Savannah		8:30 A.M. to 11:30 A.M.	Mon. March 25th
Public Exhibition - Union Station			
		12:00 Noon	Mon. March 25th
Lv. Savannah	SAL	2:00 P.M.	
Ar. Jacksonville		3:30 P.M. to 9:30 P.M.	
Public Exhibition - Union Station			
		8:00 A.M.	Tues. March 26th
Lv. Jacksonville	SAL	10:00 A.M.	
Ar. Ocala		10:00 A.M. to 12:30 P.M.	
Public Exhibition - Seaboard Station			
		12:30 P.M.	Tues. March 26th
Lv. Ocala	SAL	2:30 P.M.	
Ar. Winter Haven		2:30 P.M. to 3:30 P.M.	
Public Exhibition - Seaboard Station			
		3:30 P.M.	Tues. March 26th
Lv. Winter Haven	SAL	4:15 P.M.	
Ar. Sebring			
		4:45 P.M.	
Lv. Sebring		7:00 P.M.	
Ar. West Palm Beach			
Public Exhibition - Seaboard Passenger Station 8:00 P.M. to 10:00 PM			
		11:30 P.M.	Tues. March 26th
Lv. West Palm Beach	SAL	1:30 A.M.	Wed. March 27th
Ar. Miami			
Public Exhibition - Seaboard Passenger Station 9:00 A.M. to 9:00 PM			

The *Twin Zephyrs*, Nos. 9901 and 9902, were near replicas of the first *Zephyr* (No. 9900), with the exception of certain changes in floor plan, seating capacity, insulation, heating and air conditioning arrangement, and air brake equipment. Both were powered by 600-hp diesel-electric engines furnished by EMC of the same type as in the original. Their frontal appearance was altered somewhat by the utilization of smaller air intake grills positioned above the operator's cab. This change eliminated the cosmetic "beetle brow" that had characterized the first *Zephyr*, and the repositioning of the train's air horn from behind the grill to on top of the locomotive.

Each of the trains consisted of three articulated body sections carried on four-wheel roller bearing trucks, totaling approximately 190 feet long, weighing approximately 225,000 lbs., with a seating capacity for 88 passengers. The principal difference between these two trains and the first *Zephyr* was the elimination of the 31-foot mail compartment, something not required for the St. Paul run since the railroad did not have the mail contract between Chicago and the Twin Cities. This made the lead unit of each train slightly shorter than No. 9900, but the utilization of this space was instead for bag-

The christening ceremony for the *Twin Zephyrs* took place at Chicago's Union Station on April 15, 1935. Twin sisters Marion and Frances Beeler each broke a bottle of champagne on these two trains. *BNSF ARCHIVES*

Perhaps the most famous photograph of the *Twin Zephyrs* was taken east of Aurora, Illinois, on the day before their christening. The two trains traveled side by side from Aurora to Chicago. *BNSF ARCHIVES*

Twin Zephyr No. 9901 at St. Paul in 1934, shortly after entering service. *Jay Williams Collection*

gage and express, thus providing additional room for a larger kitchen, pantry, and lunch counter, and additional seating space to accommodate 16 more passengers—hence the additional weight.

The first car of each train, in addition to the space occupied by the operator's cab and engine room, contained a baggage compartment and a kitchen annex. In the forward end of the second car were the kitchen and the serving pantry which also served as a lunch counter. Additional provision was made for the seating of 40 passengers in individual reclining seats. In the third car were located coach seats for the accommodation of 24 passengers and a large parlor compartment for 24 passengers in comfortable individual chairs. Lavatory facilities were provided in each of the three cars.

The interior color scheme for the train was characterized by the use of plain pastel shades of green, blue and gray, blended harmoniously with the drapery, upholstery and carpets. Lighting was provided by reflected light from tubular ducts in the ceiling utilizing the principle of diffused illumination.

As the *Twin Zephyrs* served a different and longer distance travel market than

Twin Zephyr floor plan. *Railway Age*

that of the first *Zephyr*, a larger kitchen and pantry designed to provide continuous buffet or diner service for a ten-hour period was provided on the trains. The pantry contained two iceboxes, a crushed ice compartment with cooling coils for a drinking fountain, and a cold compartment for ice cream, cream and milk. The kitchen was also equipped with a range, steam tables, warming closet, coal bin, a large refrigerator, iceboxes for fish and crushed ice, an immersing sink with tabletop, and a cabinet provided with the latest four-unit coffee urn designed for railroad safety service. A cutting board and serving table were provided at the door between the pantry and kitchen, and an "air curtain" at this opening protected the pantry from the heat, odors, and gases which could potentially originate in the kitchen. Overhead storage and linen lockers were provided in all three compartments.

The pantry could provide counter service for four passengers at one time, while 16 passengers could be served in the dinette across from the pantry on removable black Formica tables. Individual trays of anodically-treated aluminum could be attached to all reclining seats in the coach compartments and to the arms

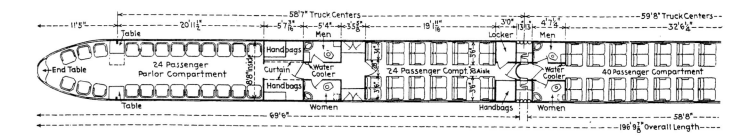

of the lounge chairs located in the observation end of the train. Removable section tables were able to be set up where opposed seats occurred at the bulkheads in the 24-seat passenger compartments.

The three passenger compartments were completely air-conditioned by mechanical equipment provided by General Electric. The compressor and condenser units were housed beneath the floor of two cars while the evaporators and distributing fans were built into the roof areas above the vestibules. Vapor type steam heat was provided by an oil-fired Peter Smith boiler with an evaporative capacity of 500 lbs. per hour. A thermostat for the control of the air conditioning radiators was located on a panel near the center of each compartment about five feet above the floor. The thermostat for the side-wall radiators was placed near the floor and served to bring these radiators into action automatically when the heat distribution from the air conditioning units was not sufficient to maintain a pre-determined temperature at the floor.

Both the side walls and the roofs of the passenger compartments were thoroughly insulated with a lightweight material designed to combine low heat conductivity with added sound deadening. Cork insulation was used in the floor construction. The windows were double hermetically sealed units, made of two pieces of Duplate, one quarter-inch thick shatterproof glass, having a one quarter-inch of dry air space in between both panes.

The prime mover of the Electro-Motive power plant was a Winton 600-hp high-compression, two-cycle 8" x 10", eight-in-line cylinder diesel engine. Power for all the auxiliary services was taken from the engine in excess of its 600-hp traction rating. Compressed air for the train was furnished by a Gardner-Denver,

75 cubic ft. per minute air compressor, with direct mechanical drive from the rear end of the engine crankshaft. This differed from the first *Zephyr*, where compressed air was provided by two motor-driven compressors of 25 cubic ft. per minute capacity each.

The four trucks were provided with Timken roller bearings on all journals. These were of the conventional outside-bearing type, with various refinements in the design to improve the riding qualities and reduce the weight and assure for quiet operation.

The train was equipped with Westinghouse air brakes which had been specifically developed for use with high-speed, articulated train units. This was an electro-pneumatic brake with straight air brake availability in case of electric failure or failure of the straight-air service brake. The electric feature, subsequently provided on the first *Zephyr*, gave simultaneous brake application on each of the four trucks at a fraction of a second sooner than was possible on the first train. The brake operation could be initiated from the brake valve in the usual manner, the valve being self-lapping, thus assuring rapid sensitivity of brake application and release.

The *Twin Zephyrs* followed the route of the Mississippi River for part of their journey. The *Twin Zephyrs* began making daily round trips between Chicago and Minneapolis on June 2, 1935. *BNSF ARCHIVES*

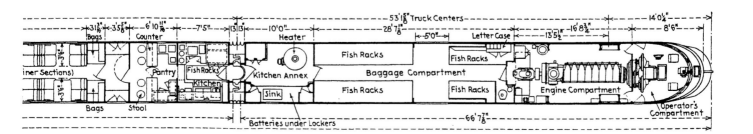

By June 2, 1935, the *Twin Zephyrs* began making daily round trips of 882 miles between Chicago and Minneapolis due to heavy demand. One of the *Zephyrs* left Chicago at 8:00 a.m., arriving at St. Paul at 2:30, and Minneapolis at 3:00 p.m. The other train operated southbound on a similar schedule. On the return trip, one train left Chicago at 4:00 p.m., arriving at St. Paul at 10:29 p.m., and at Minneapolis at 10:59 p.m., while the other twin set departed from the Twin Cities on a similar schedule.

Under this arrangement, each train traveled 882 miles per day as compared with 441 miles per day. The trains were so well patronized that they were generally sold out each day, averaging 316 passengers per day. At this point in time, in order to avoid confusion with the original *Zephyr*, the railroad changed the name of the first *Zephyr* to "Pioneer Zephyr."

In the first week of their operation, the *Twin Zephyrs* carried a total of 1,211 persons, or an average of 86 passengers per trip. The results of a questionnaire given to passengers, asking how they would have made a trip had they not used the *Zephyr*, revealed

that of the 801 persons answering, 8.9 percent would have used an automobile, 3.7 percent would have used a bus, 8.7 percent would have taken an airplane, 33.6 percent would have used some other day train, and 45.1 percent would have used an overnight train.

During their first three weeks of operation, the *Twin Zephyrs* carried 3,539 revenue passengers, or an average of 85 passengers each way daily. During the same period, 887 applications were made for seats, an average of 42 per day, which could not be filled.

Due to the large number of persons seeking accommodations on the morning run of the *Twin Zephyr* on August 3, a standard steam-powered train had to be operated as a second section operating 30 minutes behind the first section. Requests for seats on the *Twin Zephyr* were so numerous on that day that the Burlington's passenger traffic representatives were forced to solicit those who could not be accommodated to take space on the steam train. As a result, 80 additional revenue passengers were secured, or enough to ensure a profitable operation of the second section.

In point of fact, research sponsored by the Edward G. Budd Manufacturing

On December 20, 1936, the Burlington and the Alton Railroads established joint passenger service between St. Louis and Kansas City. The train chosen for the run was No. 9902, formerly one of the *Twin Zephyrs*. The new train, known as the *Ozark State Zephyr*, left St. Louis in the morning for Kansas City, making a return trip the same afternoon. The train is at Kansas City, Missouri, in this view from May 15, 1938. The original BURLINGTON ROUTE nose herald has been altered to reflect the joint operation by Alton and Burlington. *W. C. THURMAN, J. W. SWANBERG COLLECTION; BAGGAGE LABEL, EDWARD LEVAY COLLECTION*

Company revealed that the *Zephyr*s could operate on the revenue collected from 17 passengers, whereas it would require 60 or more tickets to pay for the operational cost of a conventional steam-powered train. The research also showed that the *Zephyr* trains were operating at 30 percent of the cost of steam-powered trains whereas they doubled the business that had previously been experienced.

Competition in the Chicago–Twin Cities corridor began to boom. Competitors Milwaukee Road and C&NW handled record numbers of passengers between Chicago and the Twin Cities over the 1935 Labor Day weekend, necessitating the operation of extra sections.

The *Twin Zephyrs* were operated to capacity on each run and on August 31, another steam train was operated as a second section southbound carrying 143 passengers.

The steam-powered *Hiawatha* of the Milwaukee Road was operated in two sections, both north and southbound on August 30 and 31, and September 1 and 2, while on August 31 it was operated northbound in three sections. The five sections operated on August 31 carried 1,603 on-and-off passengers.

Just to the east, the Milwaukee Road's arch rival Chicago and North Western's steam-powered *400* was operated in two sections, northbound on August 30 and September 2, while extra cars had to be added to all sections on each day from August 29 to September 2.

With the pronounced success of three *Zephyr*s in service, the Burlington was about to embark on ordering its fourth trainset, the *Mark Twain Zephyr*.

THE MARK TWAIN ZEPHYR

With the solid success of the original *Zephyr* and the *Twin Zephyrs*, the CB&Q confidently ordered a fourth trainset from the Budd Company to capture passenger traffic in the St. Louis–Burlington (Iowa) market. Serving the region made famous by celebrated humorist Samuel Clemens, the train was named the *Mark Twain Zephyr*.

After leaving the Budd Company plant on October 8, 1935, the train (No. 9903) moved from Philadelphia to New York over the Pennsylvania Railroad and in the afternoon traveled over the Lehigh Valley from New York to Bethlehem, Pennsylvania. There it was exhibited to officers and employees of the Bethlehem Steel Company (which supplied materials) and to students of Lehigh University, after which it was placed on public exhibition at the Lehigh Valley Railroad station in Bethlehem.

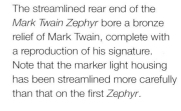

The streamlined rear end of the *Mark Twain Zephyr* bore a bronze relief of Mark Twain, complete with a reproduction of his signature. Note that the marker light housing has been streamlined more carefully than that on the first *Zephyr*.

The four-car *Mark Twain Zephyr* was the Burlington's fourth lightweight diesel-electric train. It closely resembled the original *Zephyr* and contained many of the design characteristics incorporated into the *Twin Zephyrs*. It was delivered to the Burlington at Chicago on October 12, 1935, and was formally christened at Hannibal, Missouri, on October 25. It was placed in regular daily service between St. Louis and Burlington, Iowa, beginning October 28. On October 23, a speed trial was made during which it was reported to have attained 122 mph for a distance of three miles between McCook, Nebraska, and Oxford.
BOTH, RAILWAY AGE

On October 9, it was placed on public exhibition at Wilkes-Barre, Pennsylvania, and then at Ithaca, New York. On the following day, it moved over the Lehigh Valley between Ithaca to Buffalo for transfer to the New York Central Railroad for a public exhibition scheduled at Erie that same day. On October 11, it moved over the New York Central to Chicago and delivery to the Burlington.

Before being placed in operation, however, the *Mark Twain Zephyr* was operated from Chicago to the Twin Cities and return on October 13 in a test run, covering the 882 miles in twelve hours. The next day the train was taken to the company's shops at West Burlington where the baggage car was removed to prepare for speed trials at McCook on October 23. This informal speed test of the train was made to measure the limits of endurance of the train's power plant, during which it was reported to have operated at 122 mph for a distance of three miles between McCook and Oxford.[11]

As with the other *Zephyrs*, aluminum trays could be fitted to the backs of coach seats for meal service. The coach was the third car in the train which included a kitchen compartment for dining service, and a 16-passenger dining section, with a 20-coach compartment. Note that luggage racks have been installed above the seats, a feature absent from the original *Zephyr*. Improvements such as this were made as the railroad sought to add conveniences for its passengers.
RAILWAY AGE

The 92-seat *Mark Twain Zephyr* originally consisted of four cars carried on five trucks, making it approximately 280 feet long and weighing about 287,000 pounds. Like its companion *Zephyr*s, the *Mark Twain Zephyr* was powered with an Electro-Motive 600-hp, two-cycle diesel locomotive power plant. In a departure from previous *Zephyr* orders, each of the cars and the locomotive were identified by names closely associated with the celebrat-

ed author, augmenting assigned numbers.

In addition to the power compartment, the first car of the train (No. 9903 *Injun Joe*) contained a 30-foot convertible railway mail service compartment and a 15-foot compartment for storage mail. The second car (No. 506, *Becky Thatcher*) consisted entirely of a 64-foot baggage compartment, while the third car (No. 551, *Huckleberry Finn*) included a kitchen compartment for dining car service, and a 16-seat passenger dinette section, with a 20-seat passenger coach compartment complete with mens and womens lavatories. The train also offered meal service at the passenger seats.

The fourth car (No. 572, *Tom Sawyer*) contained a 40-seat passenger coach compartment, toilet accommodations for men and women, and luggage and equipment locker space in addition to the 16-seat parlor lounge compartment at the rear.

The principal changes in this train's design as compared to the original *Zephyr*s were in the provision of additional baggage space and a somewhat revised seating arrangement. Passenger compartment interior seating included individual adjustable seats, with serving tray equipment similar to that now found on airlines. Certain changes were also made to the truck design. Additional improvements were made in the heating and air conditioning systems, including the provision of a Clarkson coil-type boiler, furnished by the Vapor Car Heating Company, designed especially for use in lightweight trains.

The five trucks which carried the train were of an outside-bearing type with various refinements in design to improve the riding qualities and reduce weight and promote quieter operation. They weighed 70,000 pounds, exclusive of the gears and motors of the power truck, and all had cast steel truck frames and bolsters furnished by the General Steel Castings Corporation. All journals were fitted with Timken roller bearings. The distribution of the train's weight was such that no two trucks were loaded alike. The power truck, for example, was estimated to carry a weight at the rails of 94,543 pounds; the first trailing truck between the first and second car bodies carried approximately 51,674 pounds; the second trailing truck between the second and third truck bodies, 56,993

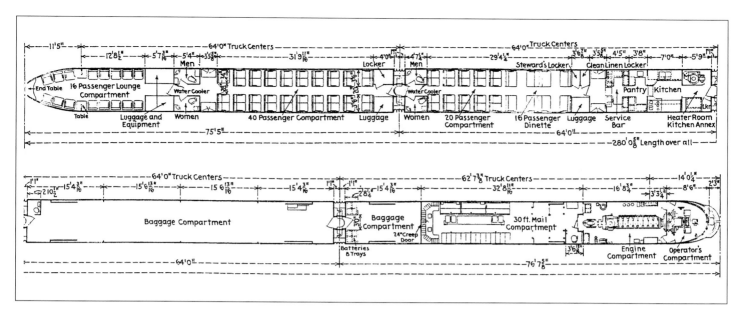

Floor plan of the four-car *Mark Twain Zephyr*. RAILWAY AGE

pounds; the third trailing truck, between the third and fourth car, 51,485 pounds; while the truck at the rear end of the train carried 32,550 pounds.

The three passenger compartments were completely air-conditioned by Frigidaire mechanical equipment. The compressor and condenser were housed beneath the floor of two cars, while the evaporators and the distributing fans were built into the roof above the vestibules and baggage locker space. This arrangement permitted ready accessibility to the apparatus for repair and maintenance.

The capacity of the train's refrigerating system was 12 tons, and in order to supply stand-by service of the air conditioning from outside sources, a 220-volt, 60-cycle A.C. motor was used to drive the compressor in the D.C. motor, which then became a generator, charging the battery.

When the train was in operation, all power was designed to be supplied from the auxiliary generator with 77-volt direct current. The entire equipment for the train weighed approximately 5,200 pounds.

Perhaps the train's most notable feature was the streamlined rear end of the observation car which carried a bronze relief of the famous humorist and a reproduction of his signature.[12] The original *Zephyr* lacked any markings in the space traditionally reserved for a conventional tail sign, and this was a bold departure from the traditional.*

On October 25, a formal christening ceremony was staged at Hannibal by Miss Nina Gabrilowitsch, granddaughter of Samuel L. Clemens (Mark Twain) and daughter of Detroit Symphony Orchestra conductor, Ossip Gabrilowitsch. The railroad's publicity office was becoming quite adept at producing these events.

The newest *Zephyr* was finally placed in service between St. Louis, Missouri, and Burlington, Iowa, on October 28, becoming trains No. 43 and No. 44. Number 43, northward, left St. Louis at 7:50 a.m., arriving in Burlington (221 miles distant) at 2:25 p.m.. Southbound, the train left Burlington at 3:20 p.m., arriving in St. Louis at 10:28 p.m.. The trains connected at Burlington with the *Aristocrat*, which left Burlington, westbound, at 3:04 p.m. and eastbound at 2:35 p.m.

With four *Zephyrs* in service, the Burlington was poised to expand the fleet. Curiously, despite the rapid and well-publicized success of the *Zephyr* trains, only one other railroad had bought into the Budd Company's *Zephyr* design—the Boston & Maine/Maine Central, which called their train *The Flying Yankee*. It was in most respects identical to the original *Zephyr* and was purchased for many of the same reasons, operating between Boston and Bangor, Maine.

The Budd Company did market the concept to other railroads, most notably the New York, New Haven & Hartford, but the cost was too great for the carrier which opted instead to purchase an articulated trainset from the Goodyear-Zeppelin Company of Akron, Ohio.

The articulated train movement was a proven design and filled a need for the Burlington, yet significant changes in the concept were in the offing. ▦

*In the subsequent reincarnations, such as the *Advance Denver Zephyr*, the train retained its distinctive markings.

Shortly after its delivery to the Burlington, the baggage car was removed for speed tests. On May 31, 1936, the *Mark Twain Zephyr* was removed from its St. Louis–Burlington run, where it had operated as trains Nos. 43 & 44, and moved to the Chicago–Denver market, serving as the *Advance Denver Zephyr*. The purpose was to initiate a new high-speed passenger service in the Chicago–Denver market in order to compete with the Union Pacific's *City of Denver*, which was due to enter service in mid-June. Here is the *Mark Twain Zephyr* operating as train No. 10, the *Advance Denver Zephyr*, being readied for its first trip on May 31, 1936. OTTO PERRY, DENVER PUBLIC LIBRARY WESTERN HISTORY DEPARTMENT

Following its brief stint at the *Advance Denver Zephyr*, the *Mark Twain Zephyr* returned to its St. Louis–Burlington route, but the articulated trains were moved around the system as operating demands dictated. In this photograph, the *Mark Twain Zephyr* is operating as train No. 19, the *Ozark State Zephyr*, on August 16, 1940, replacing no. 9902, formerly the *Twin Zephyr*. Note that the nose herald has been altered to reflect the joint operation by the Alton and the Burlington. The baggage car would be reattached in the months ahead and the engine would undergo a facelift with the addition of a large oscillating Mars light arrangement, added in the mid-1940s. OTTO PERRY, DENVER PUBLIC LIBRARY WESTERN HISTORY DEPARTMENT

THE LABOR FRONT

Naturally, the changes in operating practices which attended the *Zephyr's* use made railroad labor apprehensive that the cost savings to be realized would come at their expense. Would the economies which were inherent in the trains' design threaten the status quo of labor contractual agreements? Would new technology bring with it efficiency and thereby alter a way of life for thousands employed in providing service to an industry based on old technology?

These were serious questions for railroad labor as the Burlington (and other roads) had hoped to save on operating expenses with their new trains. Labor unions certainly weren't about to make any concessions that might entail the loss of union jobs, but railroad labor employment was falling nevertheless, from a high of two million in 1920 to about half that in 1933. The Burlington alone employed close to 30,000. Although Ralph Budd made a habit of meeting with union representatives and frequently urged conciliation and compromise, he was vexed and often annoyed by the otherwise shortsighted stance taken by unions when it came to wage demands and matters of improving productivity.

Obviously, from the viewpoint of the unions, the ideal situation was that of full employment and excellent wages, yet, as Budd observed, "in practice, as wages have been increased, employment has decreased because it was inevitable that labor costs would be controlled as far as possible by the introduction of improved methods and machines. Employees should consider thoughtfully the balance between the cost of labor, on the one hand, and the cost of labor-saving devices on the other."[13]

A controversy soon developed with the use of diesels in passenger train service on the Burlington. The Brotherhood of Locomotive Firemen and Enginemen demanded that the railroad employ a fireman in addition to an engineman on both diesel-electric trains and diesel-electric switchers, their contention being that the employment of the two men was essential to safety. The management of the railroad held that employee and public safety were not jeopardized at all when such locomotives were operated by one man and that by calling a strike, the brotherhood was trying to evade the contract which provided for a 30-day notice for changes in the existing agreements.

Thus, on December 3, 1935, the Brotherhood of Locomotive Firemen and Enginemen notified the railroad that a majority of its 1,500 members were in favor of a strike and asked for another conference with the Burlington's management. This conference took place on the following day and when the railroad would not waive its rights under the Railway Labor Act, the brotherhood set the time and date for the walkout at 6:00 p.m. on December 9. Shortly after the strike call was issued, Dr. William Leiserson, chairman of the National Mediation Board in Washington, telegraphed Ralph Budd urging mediation of the controversy.

Budd interpreted the message of the chairman that the brotherhood wished to change existing agreements which, in accordance with established custom, opened existing schedules for consideration. An issue of significant importance was about to be decided which would have a profound influence on future labor negotiations.

Although the strike of 1,500 members of the Brotherhood of Locomotive Firemen and Enginemen on the Chicago, Burlington & Quincy was scheduled to take place on the 9th, it was averted on December 8 after a conference attended by Judge James W. Carmelt of the National Railway Mediation Board; L. O. Murdock, assistant to the executive vice-president, and W. F. Thiehoff and J. H. Aydelotte, general managers of the Burlington; and M. Larson, general chairman and J. P. Farrell, vice-president of the firemen's brotherhood. As so often happens in railway labor negotiations, agreements are finally reached through compromise where one side gives something and the other gives something up. The tangled web of railway contracts of this day are the result of precedents established in the rail industry's history. In this case, a result of the compromise that was reached, the Burlington agreed that it would employ a "helper" to assist the engineman on diesel-electric streamlined passenger trains and the brotherhood would not insist that a helper be employed on diesel switching locomotives. With the use of diesel-electric technology in its formative stages, and its potential still uncertain, this seemed like a good bargain for both sides as "steam still ruled."

On December 8, in a meeting in Ralph Budd's office, both parties agreed to waive their rights and the brotherhood agreed to withhold its demands for two enginemen on switching locomotives. The management felt that while its streamlined trains were safe when operated with one man, it could not publicly contest the employment of a helper, especially in view of the doubt already created in the minds of the traveling public through the publicity that had been generated by the controversy. That publicity, implying that operation of a high-speed train by one man was unsafe, was impossible to combat.

Still, the railroad tried to counteract the impression. In its annual report, the railroad stated, "The operation of these trains is and always has been safeguarded by an automatic device known as a 'dead man's control,' which will stop the train immediately should the engineer release the pressure exerted by his hand or foot." However rational and sound an argument, it was of no use.

The added expense of a fireman on the streamlined trains not only would incur considerable increased operating expense for the railroad with the addition of 20 employees at an annual cost of an additional $50,000, but it was to set a precedent that would haunt the railroad industry for decades to come.

As early as 1936 when the railroad ordered the *Denver Zephyrs*, pulled by two separate engines, an "A" unit and a "B" booster unit, the Burlington ran head long into the issue of paying for extra crew members to "operate" a multiple diesel locomotive consist. The railroad had already acquiesced in the fireman issue on its single diesel-powered trains, but this was a different matter. Traditionally, when a train was operated by more than one steam locomotive, there was a crew aboard the second engine to operate it, i.e., an engineer and a fireman. How this would be applied to a diesel-electric powered passenger train that could be controlled from one position was uncharted territory, yet when considering union demands, almost anything was possible, no matter how irrational. When diesel-electrics started appearing, the unions tried to apply the principle to diesel combinations, demanding that an engineer be assigned to the second unit. The firemen's brotherhood likewise demanded that a fireman/helper be assigned.

EMC constructed the units so they were co-dependent, that is, the "B-unit" could not be operated independently as it contained no operator's cab, only a hostler's control stand. Due to space limitations in the "A-unit," the B-unit contained the steam boiler for train heat, making the A-unit dependent on the B-unit. Thus, the CB&Q assigned a number only to the lead unit, making the pair "one unit." Indeed, this is how the units were referenced in promotional material and in news articles. On the books, the units carried a suffix "A" or "B" to distinguish the two, but—fearing that the operating unions might insist on a separate crew for the (cabless) booster, or make claims for pay for operating two engines—nowhere was a number painted on the exterior of the second unit.

Other roads ran into the same difficulty, forcing them to employ similar tactics to avoid having to pay multiple crews on multiple-unit consists, or pay a higher wage. The issue would become of greater concern as diesel-electrics continued to proliferate, but the Burlington, meanwhile, was able to manage with the arrangement.

4 EXPANDING THE FLEET

By March 1936, the *Pioneer Zephyr*, the *Twin Zephyrs*, and the *Mark Twain Zephyr* had completed a total of 697,687 miles with 94 percent on-time performance, compared with 60 percent on-time performance for other passenger trains on comparable runs. The availability for service of the four trains averaged an impressive 97 percent. In remarks by Ralph Budd for the April 1936 issue of *Civil Engineering*, he indicated that the high availability rating was attained by careful inspection and by replacing the parts that wore out on a definite schedule. The railroad's experience demonstrated that it was necessary to establish a mileage limitation on the main driver axles of the new locomotives. Structurally, however, the

The stainless steel structural frame for *Silver King*, to be assigned to the 1936 *Denver Zephyr*, was assembled at the Budd plant in Philadelphia and then transferred to EMC's brand-new facility in LaGrange, Illinois, for installation of its diesel engine and related components. *Electro-Motive, Kevin J. Holland Collection*

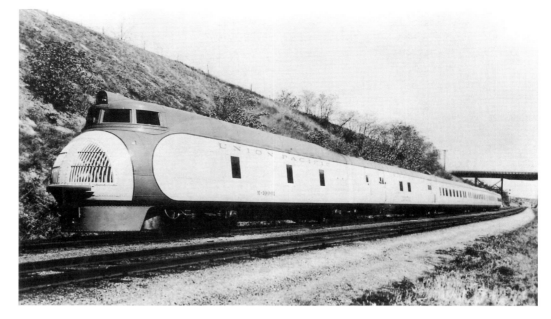

By 1936, Pullman-Standard and Union Pacific had teamed up to continue the streamline tradition with the M-10001, which included Pullman sleeping cars in an expanded version of its predecessor, M-10000. The streamline design was here to stay. *St. Louis Mercantile Library, Mark Reutter Collection*

Other railroads, such as the Illinois Central, joined the fray with their versions of streamline trains. The IC's first streamliner was the *Green Diamond* of 1936. It, too, was articulated. Perhaps one of the most famous views of the *Green Diamond* was taken near 53rd Street (Hyde Park) on Chicago's south side. *Illinois Central*

cars had proven to be "faultless." He concluded his remarks by stating that the significance of the new lightweight trains was not to be found in the comparatively small figures that they themselves represented, but rather in the idea they symbolized. In other words, they were performing work far beyond the effort expended.[14]

To nobody's surprise, the railroad had done its homework, even to the extent of building special servicing facilities at Aurora, Minneapolis, and West Burlington to maintain the trains. The *Zephyrs* required a new approach to maintenance that differed from the traditional hammering and banging to which older types of equipment were subjected. The

Burlington was ready and willing to invest in the new facilities and the training of its employees as the importance and value of the new equipment increased.

The *Zephyrs* were placed on a preventative maintenance schedule which eliminated the need to overhaul locomotives on a more frequent basis. By cycling the locomotives through the shops at intervals between 75,000 and 85,000 miles, and replacing pistons and other parts on a regular schedule, the railroad was able to keep the trains in service with most maintenance being performed during layovers between runs. General overhauls were then performed at the railroad's West Burlington, Iowa shops at 1,000,000 miles, or about every three years.[15]

By 1936, the railroad industry was filled with news of the *Zephyr* trains and the announcement that four additional *Zephyrs* would be ordered by the Burlington. It seemed only logical that the next step was to introduce trains with greater seating capacity than those currently in service. The two new *Twin Zephyrs* would be introduced with expanded services and a new train would be introduced in the company's Chicago–Denver market.

On May 31, 1936, the original *Zephyr*, now the *Pioneer Zephyr*, and the *Mark Twain Zephyr* were moved to the Chicago–Denver route and billed as the *Advance Denver Zephyr*, principally to compete with and begin service ahead of

Illinois Central's *Green Diamond* drew a lot of public attention. In this view, the train was on display at Sioux City, Iowa, penetrating the land of the Milwaukee Road.
ILLINOIS CENTRAL

Pullman-Standard recognized that it had to improve upon the tail car's design. While streamlined, the early cars from Pullman-Standard revealed their riveted construction, which was functional, but not as sleek as the Budd products.
ILLINOIS CENTRAL

Before the Burlington's *Denver Zephyr* was placed in service, the railroad attempted to stay one step ahead of its chief rival in the Chicago–Denver market, the Union Pacific. Anticipating Union Pacific's streamlined *City of Denver*, the Burlington initiated the *Advance Denver Zephyr*. In this temporary assignment is engine/train 9903, the three-car *Mark Twain Zephyr*, photographed while being serviced at Denver on June 12, 1936. Its counterpart was the original *Zephyr*, No. 9900. *OTTO PERRY, DENVER PUBLIC LIBRARY WESTERN HISTORY DEPARTMENT*

RAILROAD HISTORY *in the* MAKING

May 27 1936

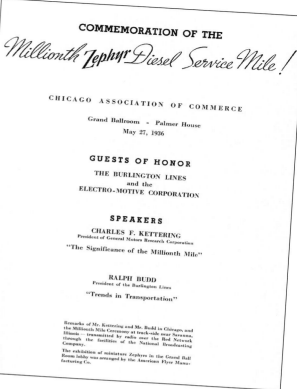

With the *Denver Zephyrs* under construction, the earlier *Zephyrs* achieved the cumulative milestone of one-million-miles' service on May 27, 1936, near Savanna, Illinois. *KEVIN J. HOLLAND COLLECTION*

The *Advance Denver Zephyr* (a.k.a the *Mark Twain Zephyr*) makes 85 mph on its first trip, east of Derby, Colorado, on May 31, 1936. *OTTO PERRY, DENVER PUBLIC LIBRARY WESTERN HISTORY DEPARTMENT*

the Union Pacific's *City of Denver*, which was due to enter service on June 18, 1936. The two CB&Q trains delivered an on-time performance of 98 percent and heralded the inauguration of the new *Denver Zephyrs*, then under construction.

The *Advance Zephyrs*, which the Burlington placed in service between Chicago and Denver on a 16-hour schedule, were filled to capacity for each trip. On several days there was a waiting list, the 60 seats in each train being insufficient to accommodate all the persons

who desired to ride the trains. Of that business it was estimated that 70 to 75 percent was through-travel.

Even at this late date, the trains continued to stir public attention. At Galesburg, Illinois, and at Burlington, Iowa, it was estimated that as many as 200 persons congregated at the station to see the trains each day.

As speed had become one of the hallmarks of the new trains, railroads strove to shorten existing schedules in the hopes that by squeezing out extra minutes spent in transit, at stations, at terminals, and through quicker acceleration, their trains would be the choice of the time-sensitive traveling public. The Union Pacific and the Burlington on July 12, 1936, reduced the eastbound running times of their Denver–Chicago streamlined trains by ten minutes, thereby placing the trains each on a schedule of 15 hours and 50 minutes eastbound and 16 hours westbound.

The *Advance Denver Zephyr* was scheduled to leave Denver at 4:00 p.m., arriving at Chicago's Union Station at 8:50 a.m., while the Union Pacific's streamliner, the *City of Denver*, was scheduled to leave Denver at 4:45 p.m., arriving in Chicago at 9:35 a.m. Under those new schedules, the eastbound *City of Denver*

would average 66.2 mph for the 1048 miles, compared with 65.5 mph for the train schedule it was replacing. The average speed of the *Advance Denver Zephyr* increased to 65.3 mph for the 1034 miles of distance, compared with 64.6 mph on the previous schedule.

During the the 97-day period between May 31 and September 5, 1936, that the *Pioneer Zephyr* and the *Mark Twain Zephyr* had operated under the name of the *Advance Denver Zephyrs*, they had operated 271,563 miles and made 264 trips with three delays being the result of mechanical failures, and arriving late at their destinations just five times. This equated to an on-time performance of 98.1 percent. A total of 14,669 passengers had been carried on the 194 trips made by the two trains.[16]

Announcements of the proposed schedule of the new *Denver Zephyr* trains and the substantial reduction in running time astounded industry observers when the schedules were compared to the then present trains in operation. Westbound, the new train was to cut 11 hours and 45 minutes from the existing schedule and, eastbound nine hours and 15 minutes. The average running speed between the two termini would be approximately 65 mph, including the seven stops en route.

THE DENVER ZEPHYRS
DIESEL POWERED   STAINLESS STEEL

OVERNIGHT EVERY NIGHT
between
CHICAGO and DENVER

SCHEDULE		
Westbound		Eastbound
5:30 pm	Lv. Chicago Ar.	8:35 am
1:10 am	Ar. Omaha . Lv.	12:45 am
1:15 am	Lv. Omaha . Ar.	12:40 am
2:12 am	Ar. Lincoln . Lv.	11:45 pm
8:30 am	Ar. Denver . Lv.	4:00 pm

THE DENVER ZEPHYR

In early October 1936 one of the two new *Denver Zephyrs* left the Edward G. Budd manufacturing plant at Philadelphia, heading for New York over the Pennsylvania Railroad on the first lap of its journey to Chicago and delivery to its owner. With a party of more than 200 professional and businessmen from Philadelphia as passengers, the ten-car train was placed on exhibition at Pennsylvania Station in New York City. Breaking with past practice, the new train was not complete-

Slumber and speed were hallmarks of the new *Denver Zephyrs*, which conveyed their sleeping cars between Chicago and Denver on an unprecedented schedule.
KEVIN J. HOLLAND COLLECTION

This builder's view of *Silver King* was taken on October 4, 1936. While the locomotive has been named, the other markings have not yet been applied. *ELECTRO-MOTIVE, KEVIN J. HOLLAND COLLECTION*

With its power plant installed, *Silver King* was placed on display inside EMC's Chicago-area facility in September 1936. *ELECTRO-MOTIVE, KEVIN J. HOLLAND COLLECTION*

Train No. 10, the ten-car *Denver Zephyr*, was photographed at Barr, Colorado, on March 6, 1937, cruising across the prairie at 80 mph. It races, without hesitation, past an old form of technology which will soon be left behind. *OTTO PERRY, DENVER PUBLIC LIBRARY WESTERN HISTORY DEPARTMENT*

ly articulated as had been the other trains. The *Denver Zephyr* consisted of ten partially-articulated body units. Because its two-unit diesel locomotives were still under construction at the Electro-Motive Corporation plant in La Grange, outside Chicago, conventional steam locomotives were used during the move to Chicago.

When the two-unit diesels were completed and coupled to the train, the new *Denver Zephyr* set a new world's record for railway speed on October 23 when the trainset (No. 9906) covered the 1,034 miles from Chicago to Denver in 12 hours, 12 minutes and 27 seconds. The average speed for the entire run was 83.33 mph, leaving Union Station in Chicago at 7:00 a.m., arriving at Union Station in Denver at 6:12 p.m.

This run, similar to that of the first *Zephyr*, was made non-stop, during which a maximum speed of 116 mph was attained near Brush, Colorado. The fastest between-station average was for a distance of 6.11 miles, at 107.3 mph.

This new run surpassed the record established by the original *Zephyr* on May 26, 1934, when that train operated between Denver and Chicago in 13 hours and 5 minutes, at an average speed of 77.5 mph, keeping in mind that the original *Zephyr* consisted of a power car and two passenger cars, compared with the two power units and six passenger cars of the *Denver Zephyr*.

The Chicago–Denver trip was sponsored by the Chicago Association of Commerce, a group consisting of business and professional leaders of the Midwest, newspapermen, and officers of the Burlington and other railways. For the return trip on the new *Zephyr*, six sleeping cars were added to the train on the 15-hour, 50-minute schedule which the all-coach accommodation *Advance Zephyrs* had been making all that summer. Despite the increased load, the train attained cruising speeds of well over 95 mph, reaching as high as 105 mph at times and arriving in Chicago only two minutes late.

During this speed trial, precautions similar to those taken for the former high speed runs were also taken. Necessary arrangements for safety were worked out at preliminary meetings with the engineering department of the railroad checking the elevations of all curves. Basic

speed charts were available from the previous *Zephyr* run and the regular schedules of that summer were used in determining safe speeds for each portion of the test run. Engineering department officers also rode the cab for the entire distance, calling the proper speeds and giving the operators the benefit of their knowledge of track conditions.

Municipalities along the route cooperated in protecting the 1,070 public and 619 private highway grade crossings which were roped off and guarded. Many of the towns along the route declared school holidays so that the children and crowds similar to the record-breaking ones that watched the original *Zephyr* pass might watch the passage of the train. Arrangements were made with other railroads to keep the interlocking plants open for the passage of the *Zephyr* as well as for keeping the Mississippi and Missouri River drawbridges closed for some time prior to the scheduled passage of the train. As a result, the *Denver Zephyr* encountered only clear signals all the way

KEVIN J. HOLLAND COLLECTION

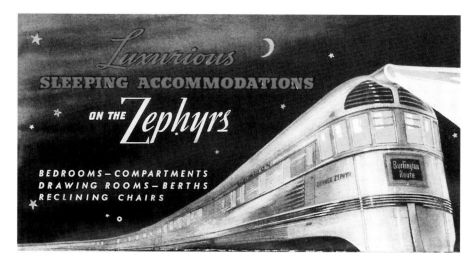

JANE GARLOW, GRANDDAUGHTER OF BUFFALO BILL
CHRISTENS THE NEW DENVER ZEPHYR
(RUNNING TIME: DENVER TO CHICAGO - 15 HRS. 50 MIN.)
SATURDAY EVENING, OCTOBER 24 AT DENVER, COLO.

The *Denver Zephyr* was christened by Jane Garlow, the granddaughter of Buffalo Bill. She christened the train while on horseback, letting loose a bottle of Paul Garrett special champagne. The date is October 24, 1936, at Denver Union Station, The stunt was repeated in Chicago on November 8. *BNSF Archives*

In the 1930s, it was not unusual to have a "Queen of the Court" at ceremonial occasions—including the *Denver Zephyr's* christening. Standing are (l-r), J. R. Van Dyke, Mrs. H. C. Leuty, Elizabeth Jane Foster, Ralph Budd, Wilma Adams, Queen Virginia Roper, Florence Collier, Beverly Peterson, and Albert Cotsworth, Jr. The queen and her court of honor were winners in the *Denver Post's* Silver Queen Contest. The locomotive crew is not just dressed for the occasion—in those days, engine crews aboard the new trains wore neckties, illustrating the new technology's contrast with steam locomotives. *BNSF Archives*

from Chicago to Denver. In addition, while the former record run was operated downhill, the westbound train climbed nearly a mile vertically en route from Chicago to Denver, and over a slightly longer route.

On November 8, the Burlington's *Denver Zephyrs* were placed in daily service between Chicago and Denver, but, contrary to popular opinion, they were not the first regularly scheduled diesel-electric-powered trains to operate between the two cities. That honor went to the Union Pacific, which initiated daily service with its sixth diesel-electric streamliner, the *City of Denver* (M-10006), on June 18, 1936.[17]

Prior to the departure of the *Denver Zephyr* from Chicago, christening ceremonies were broadcast over one of the local radio stations (WMAQ). Albert Cotsworth, Jr. made introductory remarks, with the train being christened by Jane Garlow, granddaughter of William F. Cody ("Buffalo Bill"), who approached the train on horseback and broke a bottle of champagne on the nose of the locomotive.

The train that left Denver on the late afternoon of November 8 had been christened two weeks before during ceremonies on October 24 at Denver Union Station. On that occasion, addresses were made by Ralph Budd and the Mayor of Denver, B.F. Stapleton. Miss Garlow, astride her charge, christened the train with champagne in a similar manner as she would in Chicago.

The new trains were officially Nos. 9906 and 9907. In a bold departure from its predecessors, four of the ten revenue cars were sleeping cars.

The train's capacity was 309 passengers. Each consist provided 102 coach seats, 93 upper and lower berths, 10 parlor car seats, and 104 lounge and dining seats, with 31 additional seats in the mens and womens dressings rooms. Crew quarters were provided ahead of the cocktail lounge. The first power unit contained the locomotive cab for the engineer and fireman, space for auxiliary power which would supply the 220-volt, 60-cycle, 3-phase current for the operation of lights, refrigeration and air-conditioning equipment, plus diesel-driven generators. The second was a booster unit.

Each *Denver Zephyr* consisted of six independent sections, some of which were the single-body units and others with two- and three-unit articulated vehicles, or cars. The second body unit of the train after the locomotives was a two-truck car consisting of a 23-foot baggage space and sleeping quarters for the dining car crew of twelve men. It also contained a shower room and lockers.

In the same car, to the rear of the crew quarters, was a quarter-circle bar, a cocktail lounge and a cocktail-lounge annex. The interiors were inviting. The bar consisted of a mahogany top, faced in mulberry. At its back was a peach-colored, etched, edge-lighted mirror with metal trim. The lounge was furnished with six fixed tables, two fixed curved sofas, and ten movable small chairs, the sofas and chairs being upholstered in dark tan leather. The cocktail annex, which was separated from the lounge by an ornamental aluminum grill, contained accommodations for 16 passengers at tables between transverse leather upholstered seats. The floor was covered with a light brown linoleum.

The third car body was a semi-articulated (i.e., which could be detached from the car ahead) coach seating 64 persons, with a vestibule at the forward end. The seats were of the rotating type with three-position reclining backs and removable center armrests. These seats were upholstered in a bluish green striped plush and were provided with ash trays built into the back, accessible to the persons behind. Provisions were made so that tables could be set between pairs of the seats. Windows were equipped with draperies of light olive green. Flooring was carpeted in a taupe color. Mens and ladies rooms were placed at the forward end of the car, just back from the vestibule.

The fourth car unit was a fully articulated coach seating 38 passengers. The interior appointments were different from the other cars. The seats were upholstered in henna with a two-tone striped pattern, with gold and tan draperies. The floor was carpeted in a mahogany color. Mens and ladies lavatory rooms were also provided, while in the rear of the car a separate spacious ladies lounge and annex were located. This luxurious lounge contained leather-upholstered chairs and a sofa, dressing table, electrically-lighted mirrors, wall clock, and three blue porcelain washstands.

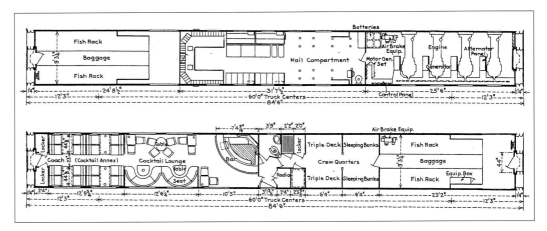

Floor plans of the ten-car *Denver Zephyrs* of 1936. *RAILWAY AGE*

Following the *Denver Zephyr's* two locomotives was the mail-express car, in this case, *Silver Courier*. The forward section of the car contained electric-generating and air brake equipment for the train. *OTTO PERRY, DENVER PUBLIC LIBRARY WESTERN HISTORY DEPARTMENT*

The fifth car unit was a semi-articulated 40-seat passenger dining car with a 23-foot long kitchen. At the rear of the car was the steward's compartment. The chairs in the dining car were patterned in comfortable leather upholstery with tables for four persons.

The sixth and seventh car units constituted an articulated pair of section sleepers (that were designed to be added or removed from the train as traffic fluctuated), each of which contained 12 sections with a mens room at the forward end and a ladies room at the rear end of the car. The seats in one of the cars was upholstered in a dark brown with a light tan figure design. The section curtains were of the traditional brown found in the then-ubiquitous Pullman sleepers of the period, as was the carpet.

In the other car, the walls and ends were colored in a dark brown and the ceiling and section partitions in a bluish tint, just for variation. The seats were upholstered in blue with tan stripes and the section curtains were colored Copenhagen blue. Although bedroom layouts were similar to their Pullman-Standard coun-terparts, the berths in the car were 1-1/2 inches longer and slightly wider than those on conventional Pullman equipment. The railroad, however, made several accommodations for "tall men" making the berths measuring 6 feet 8 inches long. A small mirror and an air-conditioning outlet was placed at the foot of each lower berth seat which was exposed only when the berth was made down. The air conditioning outlets for the upper berths were placed at the side of the overhead duct, furnished with a shutter control.

The eighth and ninth car bodies constituted another two-unit articulated vehicle, the forward one being a 12-section sleeper and the other one containing one drawing room, three compartments and six bedrooms. The section sleeper, which had mens and womens lounges, had walls and ends colored in a dark green-blue, while the ceiling and section partitions were colored a robin's egg blue. Seats were upholstered in taupe with a dark brown checkered plaid. The section curtains, as in the previous car, were colored Copenhagen blue. The carpet was a brown color.

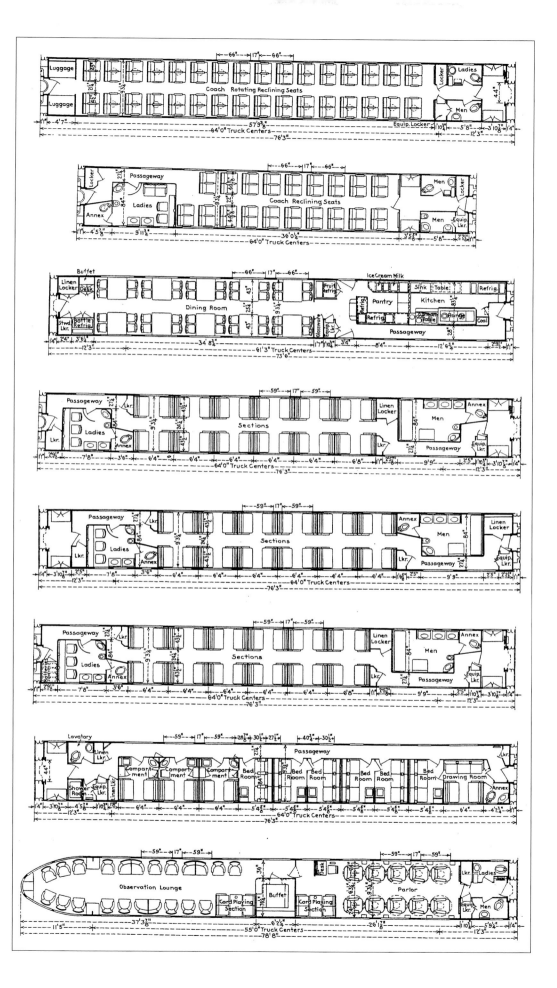

When the *Denver Zephyr* of 1936 was delivered to the Burlington it offered passengers comfortable and inviting surroundings, such as the bar lounge located in the dormitory car which was placed at the forward end of the train. *BNSF Archives*

right: In a view taken from the bar, we see the etched glass panels between the coach and bar section—common on ocean liners and in elegant restaurants of the period, and very much in keeping with this setting. *CB&Q Photo*

opposite: *Silver Lining* contained space for the express and baggage, as well as crew quarters, with the cocktail lounge and cocktail annex area located over the rear-most truck. Note the stainless steel shrouds over the trucks. *Otto Perry, Denver Public Library Western History Department*

In the all-room car, each was equipped with individual decorative treatments in which Flexwood was used with carefully selected complementary upholstery and drapes. Each room contained a small illuminated clock and an electric outlet for electric razors, curling irons, or other electric appliances, including a portable radio which could be obtained from the porter. Similar outlets and clocks were provided in all sleeper and coach washrooms. Each room was also equipped with either a toilet annex, or a fold-out toilet.

The tenth car body was a two-truck combination parlor and observation-lounge car containing a buffet, placed mid-length. The front end of the car contained ten revolving parlor chairs upholstered in fawn. The lower walls were painted a coconut brown, the upper walls sand, and the ceiling an oyster white. Draperies were of brilliant rose with white stripes and the roller curtains a fawn color. The floor was carpeted in a reddish brown border-line pattern in sand color with large spots of peach. At each end of the car, adjoining the parlor section, there was a toilet at either side. Just behind the parlor section was a writing desk with stainless steel legs and trim and two card sections of four seats each.

The observation-lounge section contained 16 single seats and three love seats upholstered in various colors and patterns. The walls and draperies matched those in the parlor section, while the oyster white ceiling contained stripes of tangerine. The woodwork of the chairs was silver-gray walnut. The floor was the same as that in the parlor section. The large windows at the sides and the curved windows at the

SILVER NOMENCLATURE

As had been the case with the *Mark Twain Zephyr*, all of the cars in the *Denver Zephyr*—including the two locomotives—were named, but for the first time all the units were given names with the prefix "Silver." Also, in an age of masculine dominance, the power units with the higher horsepower ratings were given masculine names, while the "helper" units (the "B" units) had feminine names applied. The names of the *Denver Zephyr* units were:

No. 9906	No. 9907	
Unit A, *Silver King*	Unit A, *Silver Knight*	1800-hp Locomotive
Unit B, *Silver Queen*	Unit B, *Silver Princess*	1200-hp Booster

Cars:	Cars:	
1. *Silver Herald*	*Silver Courier*	Auxiliary Engine Mail & Baggage Compartments
2. *Silver Bar*	*Silver Lining*	Coach, Cocktail Room, Crew Quarters, Crew Shower, Bath, Toilet, Baggage Compartment
3. *Silver Spruce*	*Silver City*	64-seat Coach
4. *Silver Plume*	*Silver Lake*	38-seat Coach
5. *Silver Service*	*Silver Grille*	40-seat Diner
6. *Silver State*	*Silver Skates*	12-section Sleeper
7. *Silver Tip*	*Silver Screen*	12-section Sleeper
8. *Silver Tone*	*Silver Arrow*	12-section Sleeper
9. *Silver Threads*	*Silver Sides*	Sleeper with 6 Bedrooms, 1 Drawing Room, 3 Compartments
10. *Silver Streak*	*Silver Flash*	Parlor car and Observation Lounge

Silver-series car names would go on to become a *Zephyr*—and CB&Q—hallmark, and were applied over the years to equipment owned by roads such as the Western Pacific, Denver & Rio Grande Western, and even—by dint of a solitary through sleeper—the Pennsylvania.

This interior view of the 64-seat coach reveals a marked improvement in the design and aesthetics of the coach compartments over the *Zephyrs* two years previous. *CB&Q Photo*

right: Coach windows were equipped with blinds that could be lowered and raised, in addition to decorative curtains. It made the atmosphere of the coach warm and comfortable. *CB&Q Photo*

below: Coach *Silver City* had a total length of 76 feet while *Silver Lake* had a total length of 64 feet, constructed in this manner because of physics as the train traveled through curves. These views also afford a good look at the full-width diaphragms connecting the cars. *Otto Perry, Denver Public Library Western History Department*

rear enabled passengers to view the surrounding country from all angles.

Each of the *Denver Zephyr* cars was fitted with an automatic connector made by the Ohio Brass Company. These connectors comprised air and steam, 220-volt power lines, telephone, control and signal circuits. All units were mounted beneath the Ohio Brass tight-lock couplers and the semi-permanent drawbars that were

applied in place of standard couplers between certain cars. Tight-lock couplers were placed between the two locomotive units, between the second locomotive unit and the first car, between the first and second cars, and between the fifth and sixth body units. The semi-permanent bolted drawbars were used between the second and third units, the seventh and eighth units, and the ninth and tenth units. In this manner, additional articulated units could be added to the train. The use of articulated couplings was beginning to give way to the practicality and necessity of conventional car and train design to accommodate flexibility.

Power for the air conditioning, lighting, battery charging, ventilating, blowers, refrigeration, radios, telephones, and various accessories was generated by four diesel engine-generator sets located in the first car. Each set consisted of an 85-hp, six-cylinder Cummins diesel engine which drove a General Electric 50-kw, 220-volt, three-phase, 60-cycle generator. The air conditioning equipment was made by Frigidaire Corporation, and consisted of electrically-driven compressors and condensers mounted beneath the floor of the cars with overhead thermostatically controlled combination cooling and heating units and blowers. Air distribution in the coaches, lounges, dining car and parlor car was accomplished by openings in overhead ducts which delivered the air-conditioned air through the opening between the false ceiling and the underside of the lighting duct. In the section cars, conditioned air was delivered through openings in both the side and underside of the overhead ducts and in addition, air

top: With tables set with crisp white linen and polished silverware, the *Denver Zephyr* dining car was transformed into a five-star restaurant. *BNSF ARCHIVES*

above: *Silver Grill*, the dining car, was considered with the two coaches as one articulated unit. *OTTO PERRY, DENVER PUBLIC LIBRARY WESTERN HISTORY DEPARTMENT*

left: One end of coach-dinette cars *Silver Bell and Silver Beam* contained tables for four which did not look very impressive when not set up for a meal. *CB&Q PHOTO*

top: The section sleeping cars followed the dining car. This is *Silver Skates*, lettered for Pullman, a practice not taken lightly by the Pullman Company. OTTO PERRY, DENVER PUBLIC LIBRARY WESTERN HISTORY DEPARTMENT

above: In this view, we see one of the most ubiquitous forms of overnight travel: the section sleeper. Each section had twin-facing sofas which converted into a bed; another upper berth lowered from the space above the window—hardly private, but very affordable. RAILWAY AGE

above right: The 1936 *Denver Zephyrs* offered passengers sleeping compartments unlike any that had been experienced before. The commode was located at right, while the upper berth and bulkhead were decorated in Flexwood with complementary hues of brown in the couch. RAILWAY AGE

was conveyed to the lower berth by ducts built into the section headboards.

Lighting throughout the train utilized a 32-volt system. Each car was equipped with a 5-kilovolt amp, single-phase transformer, connected over the three phases of the lighting train line so as to balance the load in each phase. In addition to the 32-volt secondary for lighting, the transformers had a 110-volt tap which supplied outlets in washrooms, drying rooms, bedrooms and compartments for electric razors and other electric accessories.

Emergency lighting was supplied from the battery. In the event that there was no 220-volt A.C. power available, a special relay circuit connected certain interior car lights and passageway lights to the D. C. train line. When the A.C. circuits were again energized, the relay was restored automatically to its former position and all lights could be operated from the A.C. power source.

The operating brake for the train was from Westinghouse, an electro-pneumatic modified high-speed control (HSC) operated by air pressure supplied by the locomotive, but electrically controlled. The trains were equipped with a retardation control which functioned at four selected speeds and operated in conjunction with speed control governors on the second and tenth trucks behind the locomotive. In order that full advantage of the braking system could be taken, the third and seventh body units were furnished with sandboxes and sanders, similar to those on locomotives, to aid in the overall braking of the train. These sandboxes were placed at the rear of lockers in these cars and occupied space which was usually of little value. The filling door was located on the outside panel and could be filled by bucket or by hose.

All the car trucks were four-wheel equalized, swing-bolstered type with

33-inch wheels on eight-foot axle centers. Each truck was furnished with four hydraulic shock absorbers to dampen the lateral swing action. Vibration and sound deadening was controlled through the generous use of special composite rubber pads located at strategic points. Journal bearings were made by the Timken Roller Bearing Company, provided with special housing covers.

Each locomotive unit built by the Electro-Motive Corporation embodied essentially welded-steel construction throughout with a stainless steel exterior and front end similar to the previous *Zephyr* trains. The "locomotive" actually

The observation lounge was located at the rear end of the last car. The Art Deco design has been carried throughout the train. *BNSF ARCHIVES*

Silver Flash was the parlor/buffet/observation lounge car. *OTTO PERRY, DENVER PUBLIC LIBRARY WESTERN HISTORY DEPARTMENT*

above: The *Denver Zephyr* also offered passengers parlor car seating. This is the parlor section located in the front end of the observation car. Note the strategically placed ashtrays from a time when smoking was still considered the height of sophistication. *RAILWAY AGE*

middle: The *Denver Zephyr* had a full 40-seat dining car in each train set. Standing at one end of the dining room, the photographer was able to get a view of the entire dining section. *CB&Q PHOTO*

bottom: The train also contained a section in the lounge car with settings of four each. Light snacks could be had for a minimal charge, which took some of the pressure off the dining car during peak periods. *CB&Q PHOTO*

consisted of two units: Unit A, which was 56 feet, 9 inches long, weighing 110 tons, developing 1800-hp; and Unit B, a 55-foot long unit, weighing 103 tons, developing 1200 horsepower.

Locomotive A contained two EMC 900-hp diesel-electric power plants, complete with auxiliaries, batteries, air compressors, and sufficient fuel capacity to make this unit wholly independent. The cab compartment was located in the forward end, with the cab's floor elevated to furnish an unobstructed view of both sides of the track. An outside entrance door was provided on each side of the cab. Cab equipment consisted of an operator's control station, complete with all the necessary controls for operating the locomotive brake valves, sander valves, etc. Adjustable upholstered seats for enginemen and a mechanic were also provided. All cab windows and doors were equipped with shatterproof glass with air-operated windshield wipers and window defrosters on the front windows. Air intake grills were located at the front end of the operator's cab and on each side of the unit at the rear end of the engine compartment close to the roof line to permit the entrance of clean air to the engine cooling blower fans. Each of the 900-hp power plants was entirely separate and complete and could be operated separately should the necessity arise.

The B unit housed one EMC 1200-hp diesel-electric power plant, also complete with auxiliaries. Two heating boilers with sufficient fuel and water capacity for the service were also included. As with the A unit, air intake grills were located on each side of the rear end of the unit close to the roof line to provide for the entrance of clean air for the cooling of the engine. This unit was also equipped with a hostler's control station to allow the turning at terminals. A toilet for the train crew was also incorporated.

Body construction was innovative, meeting all existing A.A.R. car body safety standards. There was no center sill. Buff and drag stresses were transmitted to lower cords of the side trusses through beams which substituted for the end sills of ordinary construction. The floor and all equipment were supported on the bolsters and on cross members carried by the side trusses. Outside sheathing was also supported on the trusses and carried no part of

text continued on page 78

above: *Silver Screen*, built for the *Denver Zephyr* and lettered for the *Texas Zephyr* in this 1969 view, exhibits the Ohio Brass coupling that carried the train-line electrical service as well as the brake lines. This type of arrangement was used later in the *Aerotrain* and *Xplorer*, two of Robert R. Young's "trains of the future." A. M. LANGLEY

In 1939, two additional Budd-built sleeping cars were added to the *Denver Zephyr*. They contained four bedrooms, a compartment, a drawing room, four "chambrettes," and four roomettes. The cars each had a sleeping capacity for 21.

The ladies lounge aboard one of the *Denver Zephyr* sleeping cars.

Floor plan of the 1939 *Denver Zephyr* sleepers. ALL, *RAILWAY AGE*

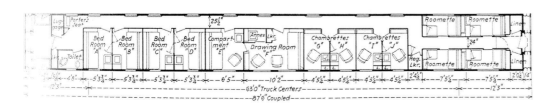

The *Denver Zephyr* is seen on its first run with ten cars at 70 mph. It was photographed east of Derby, Colorado, on November 8, 1936. *OTTO PERRY, DENVER PUBLIC LIBRARY WESTERN HISTORY DEPARTMENT*

On one of the *Denver Zephyr's* first trips from Chicago, we see a fine vista of the train being led by *Silver King*. It appears that the locomotive cab is filled with officials as well as crew. *BNSF ARCHIVES*

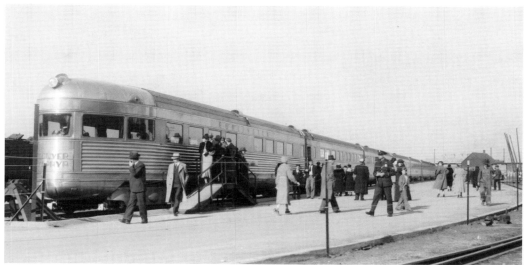

Prior to its first revenue run, the entire train was set up for public display at Denver on October 24, 1936. *Otto Perry, Denver Public Library Western History Department*

Taken from the rear of the train, we now see that the railroad has placed the name of the train in the space underneath the rear-most window. At night, this was illuminated. *Otto Perry, Denver Public Library Western History Department*

In another of the Burlington's publicity stunts, the *Denver Zephyr* (No. 9906) made a non-stop run from Chicago to the Mile-High City with six cars on October 23, 1936, in 12 hours, 12 minutes and 27 seconds. This is the train shortly after its arrival at Denver. *Otto Perry, Denver Public Library Western History Department*

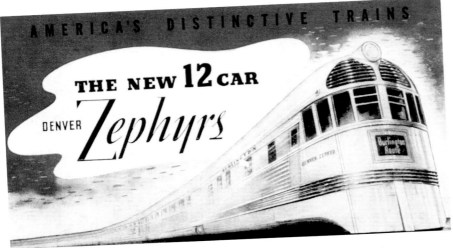

The addition of two cars to the original *Denver Zephyr* consists warranted a new brochure in 1937. *KEVIN J. HOLLAND COLLECTION*

Silver Knight and *Silver Princess* lead the ten-car *Denver Zephyr* eastbound from Denver on August 27, 1938. The departure of the train has become routine, but people still gather to watch. *OTTO PERRY, DENVER PUBLIC LIBRARY WESTERN HISTORY DEPARTMENT*

the body stresses. Although these standards conformed to the safety standards of the A.A.R., the units themselves still were unique.

Material used in the locomotive body construction consisted of high-tensile, carbon-molybdenum steel in all members where the section size was determined by stress, either actual or arbitrary, to meet the specifications of mainline railway mail service. The locomotive body, exclusive of the power plant and outside finish, weighed 30,000 lbs. and stood a static test of twice the normal load with only twice the normal deflection of 1.25 inches. The outside finish was of completely stainless steel construction which conformed with the design of the revenue cars. The stainless steel construction met and exceeded existing safety standards for rail car construction.

By themselves, the new *Denver Zephyrs* were revolutionary in design, taking streamlining and luxury train service to a higher level.

The structural strength of Budd's design was to prove itself shortly after the train was placed in service. On November 19, the *Denver Zephyr* was involved in a side-swiping incident with a Denver & Rio Grande Western passenger train in the Denver terminal.

Both the Burlington and D&RGW passenger trains were proceeding on parallel tracks, having left the station at about the same time bound for Salt Lake City. Both were traveling at less than 15 mph and as the D&RGW train reached a crossover, the switch was apparently opened and the train headed into the side of the *Zephyr*. The impact caused the rear trucks of a coach to start down another set of tracks pulling four other cars. The derailment followed. No one was hurt, but the car that was hit was a sleeping car located behind the dining car and it and the four cars following were derailed. The remainder of the train, after a short delay, continued the eastbound run, picking up two sleepers from a westbound section at

Omaha. Two weeks were required to repair the cars during which time the *Denver Zephyrs* operated with two sleepers apiece instead of four.

On the negative side, this incident demonstrated one of the flaws of the articulated train concept. Although one car may have had to have been removed from service, the potential was there for more than one car to be removed from service because of articulation, limiting the train's capacity and operation.

above: The first two units to get the enlarged headlight with an integrated oscillating Mars light were Nos. 9906 and 9907 in March of 1940. The change did not add much to the aesthetics of the engine, but it helped to increase the train's visibility. Here is No. 9906 with train No. 1 as it leaves Chicago on July 25, 1940, shortly after the installation of the new headlight unit. *Otto Perry, Denver Public Library Western History Department*

middle: While articulation was a weight-saver, it could also prove a liability when servicing or repairs were needed. Two cars might have to be removed from service even if only one needed work. Articulated 12-section sleepers *Silver State* and *Silver Tip*, in their latter *Texas Zephyr* lettering, illustrate the problem. *CB&Q Photo*

bottom: On July 12, 1940, *Silver King* was photographed at 14th Street in Chicago while being serviced. These engines would remain on the railroad's roster through the 1950s, although some were converted into "B" units. In the background is the tower of the Chicago Board of Trade. *Charles A. Brown, J. W. Swanberg Collection*

79

above: No. 4001, the second *Aeolus* (mythological Greek Keeper of the Winds), was built at the railroad's West Burlington shops in February 1938. It and No. 4000 were intended as back-up power for the CB&Q's new *Twin Zephyrs* and *Denver Zephyrs*, as the railroad lacked funds for an additional diesel locomotive. *JAY WILLIAMS COLLECTION*

middle: The first *Aeolus*, No. 4000 was rebuilt from S-4 class 4-6-4 No. 3002 and was completed on April 11, 1937. Its fluted stainless steel sides blend in nicely with the Budd equipment that follows it. Out on the plains, No. 4000 races the *Denver Zephyr* eastward near Derby, Colorado, on February 26, 1938. *OTTO PERRY, DENVER PUBLIC LIBRARY WESTERN HISTORY DEPARTMENT*

bottom: There were times when neither *Aeolus* nor the regularly assigned diesel-electric locomotives were available. On those occasions, standard steam locomotives were pressed into service to pull the flagships of the railroad. In this case, a non-streamlined S-4, No. 4003, was photographed leaving Chicago on August 11, 1939. *OTTO PERRY, DENVER PUBLIC LIBRARY WESTERN HISTORY DEPARTMENT*

THE NEW TWIN ZEPHYRS

On December 18, 1936, two new *Twin Zephyr* trains entered service between Chicago and St. Paul–Minneapolis. They replaced the two three-unit articulated trains with which this *Zephyr* service had been inaugurated in the spring of 1935. Each train was made up of a combination power-baggage-cocktail lounge unit, two coach units, a diner, and two parlor cars, the rear of which contained a small observation lounge. The train had coach seating for 120 passengers, parlor car seating for 50, including seven in the drawing room, seats for ten passengers in the observation room and card section of the rear unit, and seating for 32 passengers in the cocktail lounge and annex of the first body unit. Tables in the diner accommodated 32 patrons.

The first car in the new trains was a 76-foot, 3-inch-long unit containing an engine room in which the train power and heating units were housed, in addi-

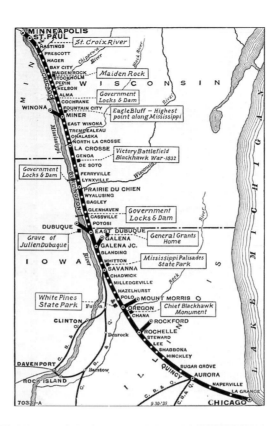

This first official photograph of the new *Twin Zephyr* was published with a press release from the Burlington's publicity representative, Joseph H. Finn. The photograph shows one of the two trains speeding towards Chicago bringing a delegation of more than 100 business and professional men from the Twin Cities to the Windy City on December 15, 1936. This was a non-stop run out of St. Paul, returning the same day. The two trains were christened in the Union Station at St. Paul and at the Great Northern Station in Minneapolis by a radio beam which released in both stations, ten miles apart, two suspended bottles of champagne. The Burlington always knew how to pull off an event. *BNSF ARCHIVES*

By the time this photograph was taken at St. Paul on September 24, 1939, the new *Twin Zephyrs* had been expanded by one car to accommodate the demand for space. *JAY WILLIAMS COLLECTION*

The Burlington made much of the new *Twin Zephyrs'* mythological car names—as well as the trains' on-board amenities and scenic route—in this 1937 promotional booklet titled "Heritage from the Gods." *KEVIN J. HOLLAND COLLECTION*

tion to a small baggage compartment and a cocktail lounge with a bar. The baggage compartment was located directly behind the engine room and separated from it by a partition. The remainder of the first car was devoted to the cocktail lounge and cocktail lounge annex, an arrangement which was essentially the same as that contained in the *Denver Zephyr*.

As with the *Denver Zephyrs*, each of the new locomotives and cars was named; instead of names beginning with *Silver*, though, one new train honored Greek gods and the other one Greek goddesses.

No. 9904	No. 9905
Locomotive *Pegasus*	Locomotive *Zephyrus*
1. *Venus*	*Apollo*
Train power, baggage, cocktail lounge	
2. *Vesta*	*Neptune*
Coach	
3. *Minerva*	*Mars*
Coach	
4. *Ceres*	*Vulcan*
Diner	
5. *Diana*	*Mercury*
Parlor	
6. *Juno*	*Jupiter*
Parlor-lounge-observation	

The second car unit was a 64-foot coach riding on articulated truck centers, accommodating 60 passengers with a womens lavatory and a mens lavatory on the right side between the forward end of the car and a stepwell at the side entrance doors.

The passenger section contained 30 transverse double reclining seats which were fitted with rubber seat cushions. The center armrests were designed to permit their being folded out of the way

HERITAGE FROM THE GODS
BURLINGTON'S *new 8 car* TWIN ZEPHYRS

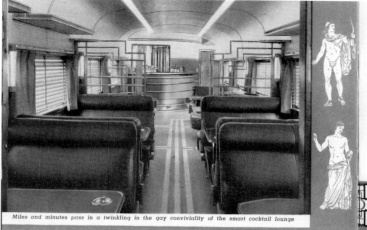

Miles and minutes pass in a twinkling in the gay conviviality of the smart cocktail lounge

COSMOPOLITAN RENDEZVOUS

*F*OR those who enjoy an appetizing highball or an after-dinner liqueur, or would while away minutes and miles with congenial friends over a foaming stein, the new Twin Zephyrs offer a gay, cosmopolitan cocktail lounge.

Here is to be found a smart, quarter-circle bar with mahogany top behind which glistens a back bar of glass and stainless steel encompassing an edge-lighted peach-tinted mirror.

Hand-buffed tan leather chairs with tubular stainless steel frames furnish informal seating arrangements for twos and threes at black-top tables, while two built-in half-moon sofas afford chummy nooks for foursomes. Separated from the cocktail lounge proper by an aluminum grille is an annex with seats for four more foursomes.

The decorative treatment of the lounge is as gay and modern as its atmosphere.

Floors are covered with inlaid design linoleum. Sidewalls are gray Harewood, the wainscoting is a rust shade and the ceiling peach. There are cheerful red-striped tan drapes and greenish-gray Venetian blinds with bright tapes and cords at the windows. Soft illumination comes from column lights in vertical fixtures, from overhead ducts, and from bulbs concealed in a cove over the bar. Music may be had from the radio-phonograph.

An expert attendant with a select stock of liquors is equipped to produce a complete variety of refreshments, while a telephone at his elbow commands instant light lunch service from the dining car and informs travelers when their tables are ready.

The cocktail lounge affords a sociable rendezvous for both coach and parlor car passengers.

Apollo   COCKTAIL LOUNGE   Venus

Carpeted floors, scientific illumination and pleasing styling distinguish the spacious coaches

SPACIOUSNESS AND ELEGANCE

*F*ORM-FITTING seats deeply cushioned with porous rubber, sound insulated walls, restfully-styled interiors and draftless air-conditioning concert to make coach passengers on the new Twin Zephyrs cozy and comfortable.

Each Zephyr carries two coaches and a dinette-coach with a combined capacity of 160 passengers. One is decorated in a restful combination of greens and complementary shades — bluish-green striped chair upholstery, floors fully carpeted in taupe, lower walls of gray-green, drapes of olive green and curtains of sea green, and upper walls and ceiling of cream. A soft, warm color harmony is achieved in the second car by means of mahogany carpeting, rust-colored lower walls, two-toned henna upholstery, golden tan drapes, and upper walls and ceiling in flesh tint. The dinette-coach, which consists of a 40-passenger coach compartment separated by a glass and aluminum grille from a dining annex seating 16, is a pleasing combination of blue and henna shades. Coach seats are reserved and individually assigned.

Seats are double-reclining, and center arm rests fold out of the way when not wanted. Windows are double width and electrical illumination is ample and diffused. Individual ash receivers are fitted into the seats in the forward coach where smoking is permitted. The two rear coaches have radio-phonographs.

Each coach has compartments for passengers' hand baggage. Men's and women's rest rooms are fitted with vitreous china wash basins and large mirrors. A coach porter and the train hostess help to make travel pleasant and care-free.

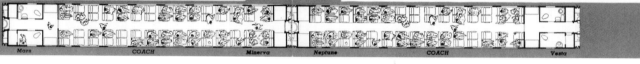

Mars   COACH   Minerva   Neptune   COACH   Vesta

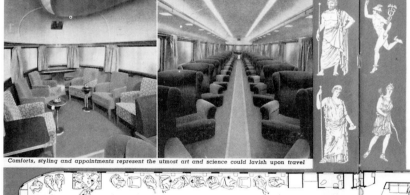

Comforts, styling and appointments represent the utmost art and science could lavish upon travel

DELIGHTFUL RELAXATION

*A*RT and science have labored together and given freely to create the two delightful parlor cars that crown the new Twin Zephyrs' passenger accommodations. Together they provide 43 commodious seats for parlor car travelers, plus a luxurious private drawing room and a congenial observation lounge.

Both cars are richly decorated and appointed. The restful fawn color of the roomy, reclining parlor chairs and the cocoanut brown and sand color of the walls are enlivened by cheery red drapes at the broad windows and a ceiling of oyster white. Illumination is ample but diffused. Large compartments for passengers' luggage and wraps, and modernly appointed men's and women's rest rooms are located in each car.

Six movable easy chairs upholstered in browns and tans in the rounded, wide-windowed end of the train, afford a vantage point from which parlor car passengers may behold the unrolling of the majestic and ever changing panoramas of the scenic Mississippi River route. The rear car, in which passengers may smoke, also contains a congenial nook with black-topped card table.

The drawing room, with private dressing room and individual radio, affords luxurious privacy for daytime travel.

The parlor cars have telephone connection with the diner for making table reservations and ordering refreshments, and are equipped with radio phonographs.

Jupiter   PARLOR LOUNGE   Juno   Mercury   PARLOR CAR   Diana

when not desired. The seats were also equipped with ashtrays that were placed in the seat backs accessible to the person riding behind. Seats were designed so that tables could be mounted between the facing pairs of seats located at the forward end of the car.

The seats were upholstered in a bluish-green striped pattern plush. The draperies were colored a light olive green. Diffused direct lighting was furnished by safety fixtures built into the underside of continuous baggage racks which extended the full length of the passenger section directly above the windows.

The third car was a fully articulated 60-passenger coach, duplicating the same floor plan as the second car. The seats

Kevin J. Holland Collection

The dining car of the *Twin Cities Zephyr* was another five-star location. Indirect lighting was provided overhead through channeled ducts. *BNSF Archives*

Passengers could also obtain refreshments in the adjoining car. *Kevin J. Holland Collection*

were of the same design as were the other appointments, although in a different color treatment. The draperies were colored a golden tan while the lower walls were of a rust color, and the upper walls and ceiling a flesh color and the floor covered with mahogany carpeting.

The fourth unit was the dining car with a kitchen at the forward end. These cars matched the dimensions of the *Den-*

ver Zephyr diners, with dining room seating for 32 with four at each table, only two tables smaller than that in the *Denver Zephyr*. The chairs were of wood construction upholstered in colored leather. The color treatment varied in the dining cars of the two trains, however. In one diner, *Vulcan*, the walls were painted blue-gray, the curtains a pearl gray, the window sills black hardwood and the

Dining is a delightful combination of colorful surroundings, attentive service and skilled cookery

MEALS TO TEMPT THE GODS

Sparkling, full-length dining cars with adjoining dinette-coaches combine alluring surroundings, attentive service and skilled cookery to provide meals that are, indeed, "fit for the gods".

Although identical in generous dimensions and fine appointments, the interior decorative treatment of the diner on each train is strikingly individual. One, the "Vulcan", has chairs upholstered in ivory leather, silver-gray carpets, blue-gray walls and ceiling, light gray Venetian blinds, and ivory trimmed buffet with blue tinted mirror. The other car, the "Ceres", has chairs upholstered in red Morocco, light chocolate lower walls and gray-green upper walls, terra cotta Venetian blinds, and matte black buffet with peach tinted mirror.

Along the sides of the immaculate stainless steel kitchen are ranges and refrigerators from which come the piping hot and crispy cold courses served in dining car and dinette at popular prices.

An ingenious "air curtain" wafts away all kitchen aromas, and special air-conditioning makes dining delightful in all weather.

Table reservations can be made from the cocktail lounge and parlor cars by telephone before proceeding to the diner.

Vulcan   DINING CAR   Ceres   Cupid   DINETTE-COACH   Psyche

Venetian blinds a light gray on the inside with silver on the outside. The chairs were upholstered in ivory colored Colonial grain leather.

The color treatment of *Ceres*, the diner of the second train, favored red and brown instead. The lower walls were colored a light chocolate with a shaded light gray-green color used in the upper walls and ceiling. The curtains were red, window sills black hardwood and the Venetian blinds were terra cotta on the inside and silver on the outside. The floor was covered with henna rust carpet bordered with peach, except in the aisle adjoining the kitchen which was covered entirely with peach-color carpet. The chairs in the dining section contained a black matte finish upholstered in red morocco leather. The kitchen and pantry were faced with stainless steel with a matte finish. The passageway adjoining the kitchen was also lined with the same type of stainless steel, unpainted, since the matte finish itself was its own reward.

The fifth car was a parlor car consisting of 19 rotating parlor chairs located in the section to the rear of the side door stepwell (the cars did not have conventional vestibules). Chairs were furnished with rubber seats and were upholstered in a fawn colored material.

At the rear end of the car was located a drawing room in which no upper berth was provided. This room was furnished with two transverse seats and a longitudinal sofa upholstered with rubber seats and covered with striped plush.

A womens room was placed on the left side of the car, forward of the stepwell and the mens room on the right. This equipment was similar to that used in the coaches. A private lavatory room was located adjacent to the drawing room, furnished with a hopper, a washstand and a dressing table.

The sixth car unit was 75 feet, 5 inches long. The accommodations included 24 rotating parlor seats, six occasional chairs in the observation lounge, and a card playing section with a table and a pair of double transverse seats. The rotating chairs were furnished with rubber cushions and were upholstered in fawn colored material, while four of the lounge chairs were upholstered in tan with a brown stripe. The seats in the card playing section were upholstered in a brown

material with a lighter stripe design. Meanwhile, the carpeting in the fifth and sixth cars was done in three colors: the field was rumba with bands of Lido sand and a center stripe of peach. The curtains adorning the windows in these two cars were red.

Both trains were essentially of the same construction and cross section as the *Denver Zephyrs* which had been delivered by the Budd Company to the Burlington several months earlier. In fact, in the interest of standardization and economy, the mechanical aspects were much the same. So, for example, both were outfitted with Frigidaire air condi-

top: *Twin Zephyr* coach interiors were very similar to those on the *Denver Zephyr*. CB&Q Photo

above: Overstuffed chairs were provided in the observation lounge at the rear of the train in different patterns. The arrangement of the lounge differed somewhat from that in its counterpart, the *Denver Zephyr*. CB&Q Photo

TWIN *Zephyr* SERVICE TWICE A DAY

Route of the TWIN *Zephyrs*

DIESEL-POWERED for smooth, effortless speed

ARTICULATED CARS for velvety stops and starts

STAINLESS STEEL strongest of all modern alloys

NON-FROST WINDOWS for clear view of scenic route

RUBBER CUSHIONED trucks for easy quiet riding

TICKET OFFICE
Phone WABash 2345
179 W. Jackson St.

Burlington Route

UNION STATION
Phone WABash 2345
Jackson Blvd. & Canal St.

In a view from May 9, 1937, we see train No. 23 led by *Zephyrus* as it travels westbound entering Aurora, Illinois, at approximately 70 mph. *TLC COLLECTION*

tioning equipment arranged in the same manner and form as that in the *Denver Zephyrs*, as well as with Westinghouse electro-pneumatic modified HSC air brakes operated by air pressure supplied from the locomotive.

The locomotives were identical with the first units of the locomotives built by EMC for the *Denver Zephyr*, and for that matter were interchanged when necessary. Each was equipped with two 900-hp, two-cycle diesel engines directly connected to General Electric generators which drove two motors on each of the two swivel trucks. The locomotive was 58 feet, 1 inch long with trucks placed on 34-foot centers, weighing 222,520 lbs.

The locomotive itself contained no heating plant, as the heating boilers were included in the train and power plant at the front end of the first revenue body unit. The 9906B and 9907B units were equipped with a pair of Clarkson CA4160 steam boilers, each capable of producing 1600 pounds of steam per hour—the boilers for the *Twin Zephyrs* were located in the power car.

The locomotive and cars were connected by Ohio Brass tight-lock couplers.

As the railroad had experienced with the first *Zephyr*, the fixed consist limited the train's capacity and it was necessary to add an additional coach to accommodate demand for space not long after the train's inauguration. Another issue related to its fixed consist was that if the locomotive or cars had to be taken out of service for maintenance or repairs that could not be accomplished in a timely fashion, the entire train had to be removed from service. This was a serious drawback.

Another problem, though a minor one, was the trains' name. Although known as the *Twin Zephyrs*, they quickly became the *Morning Zephyr* and the *Afternoon Zephyr* in order to avoid confusion since both trains were making daily round trips between Chicago and the Twin Cities.

The Chicago, Burlington & Quincy was striding ahead modernizing its passenger fleet with Budd coaches and dining cars. In February 1937, subsidiary Fort Worth & Denver ordered four 52-seat coaches from Budd, and more cars were to be ordered for the two subsidiaries over the next three years. But the Burlington had learned an important lesson: the

With the *Twin Zephyrs* each performing a round-trip per day, there had to be a name change to differentiate the two. The trains were designated *Morning* and *Afternoon Zephyrs*. Train No. 21, the *Morning Zephyr*, is leaving Chicago for its run to St. Paul and Minneapolis on August 11, 1939. Soon new E5 diesel-electrics will be replacing these early units. *Otto Perry, Denver Public Library Western History Department*

In this photograph, the *Afternoon Zephyr* is overtaking train No. 37, the overnight *Denverite*, being led by S-4 No. 4002 as they leave Chicago on August 10, 1939. *Otto Perry, Denver Public Library Western History Department*

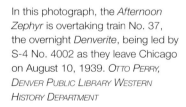

In July 1943, *Zephyrus* has been taken off its assignment as power for the *Twin Zephyr*. It is leading the day's *Denver Zephyr* at Denver Union Station, but does not look out of place even though it is not the regularly assigned power for this train. The beauty of these units lay partially in their versatility. *Harold K. Vollrath Collection*

above: The early *Twin Zephyrs*, Nos. 9901 and 9902, became the *Sam Houston Zephyr* and *Ozark State Zephyr*, respectively. No. 9901 was photographed at Dallas, Texas, in June 1938. The short three-car train was a Burlington/Rock Island Railroad joint operation, operating between Houston, Dallas, and Fort Worth, Texas. *HAROLD K. VOLLRATH*

lower left: In another view of the *Sam Houston Zephyr*, it is caught while traveling on the Fort Worth & Denver. *J. W. SWANBERG COLLECTION*

lower right: At Irving, Texas, we see No. 9901 operating as the *Sam Houston Zephyr* in March 1940. *HAROLD K. VOLLRATH*

And what happened to the two three-car *Twin Zephyrs* after being bumped by the new six-car trains? During the period that the ten-car *Denver Zephyr* arrived in October and was test-run on the Chicago–Twin Cities route, one of the three-car *Twin Zephyrs* trains (No. 9901) was shipped to Texas to become the *Sam Houston Zephyr*, a Burlington/Rock Island joint operation which became the first diesel-electric streamlined train in the Southwest. This train operated between Houston, Dallas, and Fort Worth.

When the two new ten-car *Denver Zephyrs* entered service between Chicago and Denver in November, the original *Pioneer Zephyr* returned to its Lincoln–Kansas City run, while the *Mark Twain Zephyr* was transferred to the Chicago–Twin Cities route. On December 18, 1936, with the inauguration of the two new *Twin Zephyrs*, six cars each, the *Mark Twain Zephyr* returned to the St. Louis–Burlington run.

On December 20, 1936, the Chicago, Burlington, & Quincy and the Alton Railroad established service between St. Louis and Kansas City. This was train No. 9902, released from the Twin Cities service on December 18, now known as the *Ozark State Zephyr*. Its schedule called for it to leave St. Louis at 8:30 a.m., arriving at Kansas City at 2:00 p.m. On the same-day return trip, it was scheduled to leave Kansas City at 4:00 p.m., arriving in St. Louis at 9:30 p.m.—covering the 279-mile trip in five and a half hours.

Other changes followed. The 9903 became the *Ozark State Zephyr* in September 1938, while the 9902 became the *Sam Houston Zephyr* from November 1938 to June 1939. In June 1939, No. 9902 became the *Texas Rocket*, replacing No. 9901, which returned to its *Sam Houston Zephyr* assignment.

articulated train served its purpose in a time and place. Now the company needed the flexibility afforded by the design of conventional equipment.

Three years were to elapse before the Burlington ordered its next train set, however, although five conventional coaches and three dining cars were built for the Burlington and its subsidiary Colorado & Southern in October 1937.

The next *Zephyr* would combine the elements of its forebears and the Budd Company's new conventional equipment.

GENERAL PERSHING ZEPHYR

Breaking with its articulated tradition, the Burlington introduced a lightweight, four-car train called the *General Pershing Zephyr*, inaugurated in a ceremony at St. Louis on April 20, 1939. Motive power for the new train was a 1000-hp, V-12 Model 567 EMC diesel-electric, powering a three-axle, six-wheel truck.* The company had recognized the need for versatility, yet desired to retain the appearance of its *Zephyr* fleet for the sake of uniformity.

The unit (No. 9908) was a departure for the railroad, and in some ways the unit was a pioneer. Electro-Motive by this time had experienced some problems with four-axle non-articulated passenger diesels, mostly "hunting" of the forward truck, a habit of the truck to move laterally while in motion, if track conditions were not optimum. The problem was worse with locomotives of a longer wheelbase. As No. 9908 had an overall length of 80 feet, 4 inches, the solution was to be found in a power truck of a longer wheelbase, a design by one of EMC's engineers, Martin Blomberg. The "A1A" truck carried two traction motors with a wheelbase of 14 feet, 6 inches, riding on 36-inch wheels. It quickly became EMC's standard.[18]

Instead of being completed at EMC's plant in LaGrange, the unit was assembled at the Budd plant and then shipped to EMC for the installation of the motive power unit. All electrical components were now manufactured by EMC instead of being contracted out to suppliers such as Westinghouse or General Electric. The engine had a water capacity of 540 gallons for the steam heat unit, plus a 630 gallon fuel capacity, both tanks carried underneath the locomotive.[19]

The engine's carbody was designed to integrate cosmetically with the stainless steel coaches built by Budd, with tighter fitted fluting above the window line and

* The "567" designation referred to a cylinder displacement of 567 cubic inches.

Silver Charger was a one-of-a-kind locomotive. Motive power for the new *General Pershing Zephyr* was a 1000-hp EMC diesel-electric, powering a three-axle, six-wheel truck. The unit was built by Budd, with the carbody sent to EMC for installation of the powerplant. The *General Pershing Zephyr* locomotive would prove to be among the most versatile units of the shovel-nose design—and also the last. *ELECTRO-MOTIVE, KEVIN J. HOLLAND COLLECTION*

39-3035

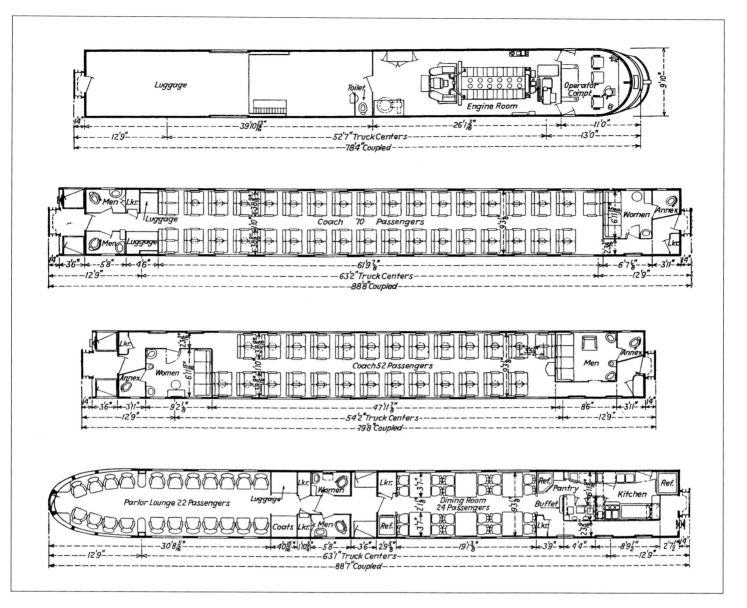

above: Floor plans of the *General Pershing Zephyr's* locomotive and three cars. *Railway Age*

wider-spaced fluting below. The engine also carried the name of the train on the flanks of its nose, painted red.

The new train entered service between Kansas City and St. Louis, operating as train Nos. 32 and 33, making a daily round trip of 558 miles. Scheduled to leave Kansas City at 9:00 a.m. and arrive at St. Louis at 2:00 p.m., it would leave St. Louis one hour later, arriving at Kansas City at 8:00 p.m. The running time of five hours included five regular stops and three conditional stops, with an average speed of 55.8 mph.

The *General Pershing Zephyr* provided facilities for daylight operation, complete with dining and lounge service, and coach seating for 122 passengers. The locomotive contained space for a 40-foot baggage room, a concept similar to the

first *Twin Zephyrs*. Two of the cars were coaches, the first of which had seats for 70 passengers, with a womens lounge at the front end and two mens toilets located on opposite sides of the aisle at the rear of the car. The train's second coach contained seats for 52 passengers, as well as contained mens and womens lounges, one at each end. Each of the passenger coaches contained a vestibule at one end of the car.

The last car in the train was a diner-observation lounge. At the forward portion of the car was a kitchen and pantry. The dining room contained three double tables on each side of the aisle, seating 24 persons. The parlor observation section at the rear of the car contained loose chairs for 22 persons. (Anticipating greater demand and an expansion of service,

text continued on page 94

opposite: *Silver Charger*, inside the EMC plant. *Electro-Motive, Kevin J. Holland Collection*

overleaf: The *General Pershing Zephyr* was inaugurated on April 20, 1939, in ceremonies at St. Louis. The 1000-hp diesel-electric locomotive was an imposing figure, with the train's name emblazoned in red on its flanks. *Silver Charger* was named after Pershing's horse. Ralph Budd spoke to the assembled crowd, as well as to a radio audience. A bottle of champagne was cleverly suspended from above for the ceremonial christening. *BNSF Archives*

The *General Pershing Zephyr* consisted of the power unit, *Silver Charger*, two coaches, and a diner-parlor-observation. Three additional cars of this type were ordered in late 1939 and early 1940 in anticipation of expanded service. In this view we see the new train during one of its exhibition/publicity trips, taken on the Burlington's Chicago suburban territory near Lisle in April 1939. The *Silver Charger* would be replicated, to some extent, a little over 60 years later by Amtrak—in the form of a powerless cab unit with baggage compartment capacity for push/pull operation. *BNSF Archives*

three additional cars of this type were ordered in late 1939 and early 1940.)

Each of the cars was named in a military motif: the locomotive unit was named *Silver Charger*, after the General's horse, with the coach cars being named *Silver Leaf* and *Silver Eagle*, and the diner-parlor-observation, *Silver Star*.

Two of the innovations which set the new train apart from the others were the use of fluorescent lighting and disc-type brakes. In addition to the general lighting, there were ten blue night lights recessed at even spaces into the center lighting fixture in the car. The lounge and dining sections of the diner-lounge also had continuous central lighting fixtures.

The interior decor of the passenger coaches had ceilings finished in light sandstone, down to the luggage racks. In the 70-passenger coach, the luggage racks and the sides and end walls to the floors were a mountain brown, while in the

52-passenger coach they were a nut pine. The floors in both coaches were covered with Chase Seamloc carpet, colored in henna rust with a mixture of mahogany. The mohair upholstery in one car was brown while in the other car it was rust. The decorations of the dining room were simple in that a single color was used throughout the room for the ceilings, walls and ends. This was a flesh-tinted light drab. The carpet was colored a henna rust, with an insert pattern colored in sand.

The styling and coloring of the interiors of the passenger carrying cars were developed by famed artist Paul Cret, who played an important role in the artistic appointments which were incorporated into the Cincinnati Union Terminal project. Photographs of these cars dramatically illustrate the improvements made over the period since the introduction of the first *Zephyr* only five years before.

The observation lounge was quite different in treatment from previous models. *BNSF ARCHIVES*

Silver Charger was more like a standard Budd baggage car outfitted with a locomotive cab on one end. Because of its greater power and flexibility, it was assigned various duties from time to time. One such occasion was serving as the lead unit for a special train for Crown Prince Frederic and Princess Ingrid of Denmark, photographed east of Denver on April 18, 1939. The coach and observation car were part of the *General Pershing Zephyr* consist. *M. McCLURE, DENVER PUBLIC LIBRARY, WESTERN HISTORY DEPARTMENT*

On June 10, the run of the *General Pershing Zephyr* was extended to Lincoln, Nebraska, where it connected with the *Exposition Flyer* for San Francisco. A St. Louis–San Francisco standard Pullman sleeping car was added to the consist of the *General Pershing Zephyr*, while one of the stainless steel reclining chair cars was operated through to Denver on the *Exposition Flyer* from Lincoln.

On the return trip, the schedule of the *General Pershing Zephyr* was adjusted so that it could pick up the St. Louis sleeping car and reclining chair car upon the arrival of the *Exposition Flyer* from San Francisco. With this added equipment, the *General Pershing Zephyr* was still able to maintain its five-hour schedule between St. Louis and Kansas City. The train's departure time from St. Louis was adjusted to 2:15 p.m. instead of 3:00 p.m., arriving in Kansas City at 7:15 p.m. instead of 8:00 p.m., with arrival at Lincoln at 11:55 p.m. Returning, it left Lincoln at 3:30 a.m., Kansas City at 8:00 a.m., arriving in St. Louis at 1:00 p.m.

The *General Pershing Zephyr* was not the last *Zephyr* to be ordered by the railroad. However, the trend now for the Burlington was to move away from the articulated train design. Meanwhile, as demonstrated earlier, the Burlington was not the only pioneer in the business. The

"Rebels" of the Gulf, Mobile & Northern held the distinction of being the first diesel-electric trains with separate power and cars, introduced in the spring of 1935. The *Denver Zephyr* of 1936 was a pioneer of a different sort—a transitional type of train. The design was an attempt to claim the benefits of articulation as well as those of conventional equipment. To nobody's surprise the novel design proved successful, but it was not repeated.

A NEW GENERATION OF TRAINS

By the end of 1936, other railroads such as the Baltimore & Ohio, Rock Island, and Santa Fe had diesels pulling their streamlined trains. The diesel revolution was well underway. Mid-way through what seemed like an interminable economic crisis, the railroad passenger business also seemed to be experiencing a revolution as traffic was on the rebound.

The revenue picture for the Burlington was improving, even when one considered the increasing truck and bus competition. In 1936, revenues for the Burlington's passenger business increased by 18 percent. In 1937, passenger revenues increased again by 18 percent.

In September 1939, the railroad confidently placed an order for a tenth *Zephyr*, (the *Silver Streak Zephyr*), a five-car

By 1940 the Burlington was ordering new EMC E5 locomotives, outfitted with stainless steel fluting, names, and nose decoration which represented the cab windows, headlight, and grill arrangement of the first *Zephyrs*. *Silver Racer* and B-unit *Silver Steed* were built for the *Texas Zephyr* in 1940. *ELECTRO-MOTIVE, KEVIN J. HOLLAND COLLECTION*

diesel-electric-drawn streamliner to be placed in operation on a daily round trip between Lincoln and Kansas City, via Omaha. It would supplant the original *Pioneer Zephyr* which would be reassigned. The new train comprised a 2000-hp diesel-electric locomotive and a train consisting of a 72-foot combination mail-baggage car with a 30-foot railway post office, a baggage express car, two chair cars containing 52 seats each, and a diner-observation car containing 24 dining seats and a parlor section, seating 22.

Subsidiary Fort Worth & Denver and the Colorado & Southern placed orders for two *Texas Zephyrs* in February 1940. The trains were pulled by two diesel locomotives equaling 4000-hp built by EMC, pulling a mail express car, baggage coach, two coaches, and a diner-observation lounge car, all built by the Budd Company.

The Burlington also placed an order with Budd for 13 stainless steel passenger cars, including two diner-observation lounge cars, nine 52-seat coaches, and two baggage cars. All were separate conventional (i.e., non-articulated) cars to be used on its principal routes.

Following on December 11, 1940, the *Ak-Sar-Ben Zephyr* was inaugurated. ("Aksarben" was Nebraska spelled back-

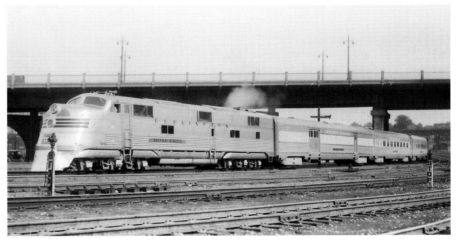

wards, but the train was named after the 1930 heavyweight train that honored the "Knights of AkSarBen," a semi-public organization dedicated to maintaining high ideals and developing progress and prosperity in the Cornhusker State.)

The *Ak-Sar-Ben Zephyr* comprised lightweight and standard passenger cars, and was placed in operation between Lincoln and Chicago. The schedule called for a running time of nine hours and one minute for the 551 miles. The train was scheduled to leave Lincoln at 11:00 a.m., Omaha at 12:01 p.m., arriving in Chicago at 8:01 p.m.

Brand-new E5A *Silver Arrow* poses at the builder in 1941. *ELECTRO-MOTIVE, KEVIN J. HOLLAND COLLECTION*

Silver Pilot is E5A No. 9911, leading train No. 22, the *Morning Zephyr*, photographed at St. Paul, Minnesota, on July 26, 1940. Trailing are cars from the latest order received from the Budd Company. *OTTO PERRY, DENVER PUBLIC LIBRARY WESTERN HISTORY DEPARTMENT*

Overnight streamline train service between St. Louis and St. Paul-Minneapolis in joint operation between the Burlington and the Chicago, Rock Island & Pacific began on January 7, 1941. The two diesel-powered trains operated jointly over the Burlington between St. Louis, Missouri, and Burlington, Iowa, and over the Rock Island between Burlington and the Twin Cities. The train's name was the *Zephyr-Rocket*, with equipment provided by both railroads. The train consisted of a mix of streamlined and modernized heavyweight cars.

Each of these trains was drawn by a 2000-hp diesel-electric locomotive (Burlington provided a stainless-steel-clad E5A, No. 9913, *Silver Wings*. Rock Island provided EMD E6A No. 627), and

in addition to the baggage and express cars, consisted of a chair car, a standard Pullman, and a dining-observation-lounge car. The railroad had decided to buy locomotives that were of more conventional "mass-produced" design.

Passenger locomotives utilizing six-wheel trucks were becoming standard power for other roads. The Burlington had experienced tragic collisions involving the deaths of locomotive crew members, one of which was the collision of the *Pioneer Zephyr* on October 2, 1939, when the train ran through an open switch at Napier, Mo., colliding at 50 mph with a stationary local freight. Both the motorman and the road foreman were killed. The implication was clear—there had to be a design change.

The railroad signed an agreement with the Brotherhood of Locomotive Engineers that effectively ended the purchase

The *Zephyr-Rocket* was a joint offering of the Burlington and Rock Island railroads between St. Louis and the Twin Cities. This 1941 brochure helped launch the train.
EDWARD LEVAY COLLECTION

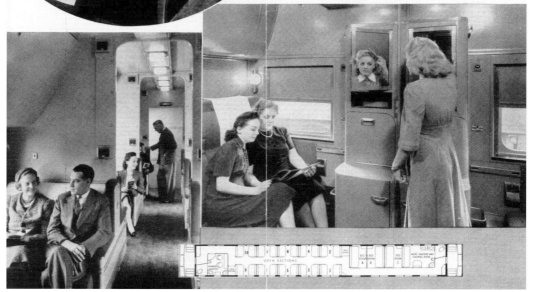

of future "shovel-nosed" engines. Since May of 1937, EMC had been selling six-axle power to the Baltimore & Ohio, and starting in 1940, the Burlington would be ordering custom styled locomotives (E5s) for its expanding *Zephyr* fleet.

The Burlington-Budd combination had proven to be an attention-getter, and their new trains had elevated service standards so that other railroads in the region knew they had to meet or exceed them in order to remain competitive.

While other railroads had been reluctant to purchase Budd cars in large quantities, they were not averse to seeking an alternative to the traditional supplier of most passenger equipment, Pullman-Standard. In fact, with the introduction of Budd sleeping cars on the market, the gauntlet had been cast in Pullman's direction. It was a challenge that Pullman could not ignore.

Even as the shovel-nosed, articulated *Zephyrs* were being eclipsed by newer and larger equipment designs, the Burlington's fleet continued to rack up astonishing mileage. The five-year-old *Pioneer Zephyr* became a "million-miler" near Council Bluffs, Iowa, on December 29, 1939. The Burlington was never one to pass up a promotional opportunity.
KEVIN J. HOLLAND COLLECTION

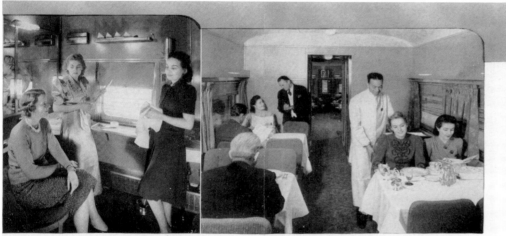

DRESSING ROOMS are unusually light and commodious in Zephyr-Rocket chair cars and Pullmans. Here is found every facility for the toilette, including outlets for 110-volt AC electrical appliances, broad mirrors, spotless washbowls.

DINING is an event on the Zephyr-Rockets, pleasing surroundings combining with delicious cuisine and impeccable service to assure extraordinary dining enjoyment at most reasonable prices.

The route of the Zephyr-Rockets is both scenic and historic. Between St. Louis and Burlington it hugs the wooded, palisaded shores of the broad Mississippi, thorofare of Indian, explorer, trapper, missionary and trader since the dawn of history. The northern sector lies through the fertile, substantial farmlands of Iowa and Minnesota, dotted here and there by lakes and attractive towns and cities.

While the Zephyr-Rockets' fast, overnight schedules are ideal for commercial travel, they are likewise especially convenient for the summer vacationist en route to the Minnesota lakes or Northwoods, or the winter traveler hurrying to the balmy Southland that lies beyond St. Louis.

Enjoy this fast Zephyr-Rocket service whenever or whyever you travel between St. Louis and the Twin Cities . . . **no extra fare.**

PULLMANS on the Zephyr-Rockets offer double bedrooms, an innovation in the St. Louis-Twin Cities service, as well as beautifully appointed sections.

THE OBSERVATION-LOUNGE with its restful, individual chairs, radio, magazine library and buffet service is an inviting gathering place for Pullman passengers as well as those desiring parlor car accommodations.

5 UNITED STATES v. PULLMAN

With the introduction of Budd-built sleeping cars into the sleeping car market—a market dominated by the Pullman conglomerate—the Pullman companies were faced with a competitor that could substantially diminish its influence and leverage. When the Burlington introduced sleeping cars into its semi-articulated *Denver Zephyr* of 1936, the new shiny cars were ironically lettered for Pullman who, by contract, was providing service to the railroad and its sleeping car patrons.

While not happy with the arrangement, Pullman did make allowances for the operation of these cars in its contract with the railroad, but the company raised issues of safety because of the stainless steel construction which

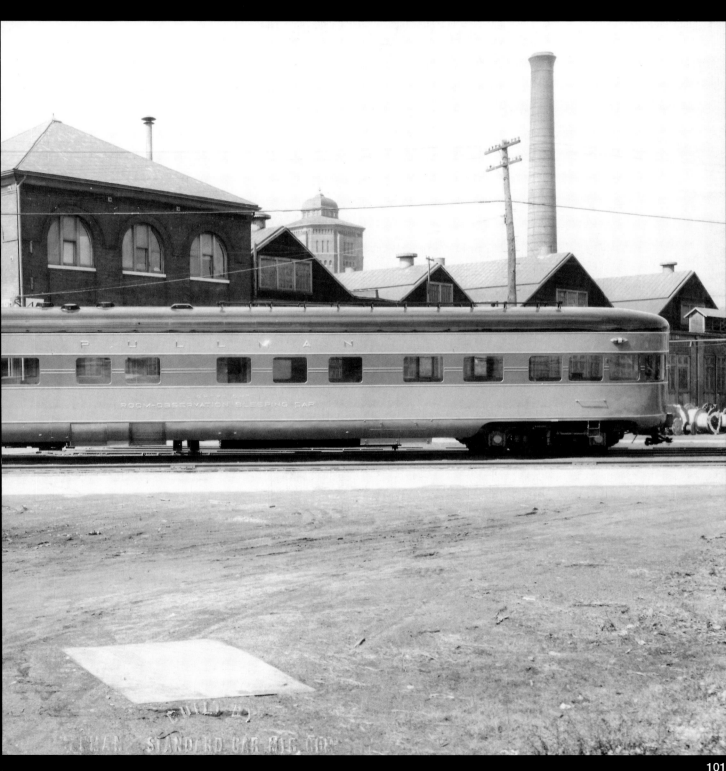

differed from its own construction methods, going so far as to demand indemnification for loss of life or injury should the cars be involved in a wreck. This turned out to be just one of many issues raised by the Pullman Company when negotiating contracts with the railroads utilizing the services provided by the Pullman Company in sleeping cars made by Budd.

Another tactic the Pullman Company utilized was to suggest that should a contracting carrier purchase or lease the sleeping cars of a builder other than Pullman-Standard, the Pullman Company might consider the contract as nullified, again due to safety requirements in the construction of the cars. With so many sleeping cars in interline service, any railroad's sleeping car services would be severely impacted and no railroad operating sleeping cars in large numbers could afford to risk such a forfeiture. While Budd had made a proposal to New York Central for an all-stainless steel *20th Century Limited* in 1938, the order went to Pullman-Standard. Cost may have been a factor, but so may have the threat that Pullman would not honor the terms of its contract with the railroad to provide sleeping car service.

What resulted from Pullman's tactics was one of the most famous legal challenges brought against the railroad industry by the Justice Department of the United States. The suit, filed in United States District Court at Philadelphia, alleged that Pullman, Inc. operated a monopoly to the detriment of its competition.

The anti-trust suit (Civil Action No. 994) was first filed on July 12, 1940, and re-filed in amended form on July 22, 1941. Named as defendants were Pullman, Inc., its wholly owned subsidiaries, the Pullman Company (operator of sleeping car service), Pullman-Standard Car Manufacturing Corporation, and Pullman Car & Manufacturing Corporation of Alabama, which leased car manufacturing facilities to Pullman-Standard, and 31 directors and officers of those companies.

"This case arose by reason of the complaint of a competitor." Thus, Seth W. Richardson, a lawyer for Pullman, expressed his version of the origin of the federal government's anti-trust suit against the Pullman organization. The trial opened in United States District Court on November 3, 1941, before a spe-

cial three-judge court composed of John Biggs, Jr., H. F. Goodrich, and Albert Maris. In response, Special Assistant to the Attorney General Fowler Hamilton denied that the suit was instituted on behalf of any private party, adding that, even if it were true, it would have no relevance to the government's right to prosecute an unlawful condition. He was upheld in his contention by Presiding Judge Biggs who held that, "the motive is not pertinent; the question is whether there has been a violation of the law."

Allegations specified in the amended complaint, all of which were categorically denied by Pullman, were as follows: 1) "Defendants have secured a complete and unlawful monopoly of the business of operating sleeping car services and interstate commerce over the railroads of the United States; 2) prices and terms charged by the defendants to railroads for sleeping car service have been non-competitive; 3) prices and terms charged by the defendants to the traveling public for services operated by the defendants have been non-competitive; 4) the defendants have secured an absolute monopoly over the business of manufacturing sleeping cars; 5) defendants have unlawfully restrained competition in the manufacture, sale, lease and distribution of sleeping cars and other types of passenger equipment; 6) defendants have forced railroads to pay non-competitive prices for rolling stock; 7) defendants have unlawfully coerced and restrained railroads in the operation of their businesses and have unlawfully forced railroads to refrain from responding to the forces of competition; 8) defendants have stifled competition in the manufacture, sale, lease, and operation of modern, lightweight, streamlined, high-speed trains and rolling stock and defendants have unlawfully retarded the growth and development of a supply of modern passenger coach and sleeping cars in the United States."

In presenting his case, Fowler Hamilton declared that the government was taking five distinct positions in its case, believing that if it were successful in sustaining any one of those questions, "it would be sufficient to sustain its case as a whole." The government's chief position was that the defendants had monopolized the business of furnishing and operating sleeping cars and of manufacturing sleeping cars which was a violation of the law regardless of the manner in which control was secured or had been exercised. "I will endeavor to show that the defendants acquired this power through the acquisition of all their competitors and finally acquired complete power over the business of manufacturing sleeping cars. No one else in the United States, although there are a number of others who are equipped and could manufacture sleeping cars, can find a market. They have no one to whom they can sell." There, in a nutshell, was the issue.

The remaining four positions were that, 1) the requirement that every road deal exclusively with Pullman; 2) control over prices at which they will furnish cars and service; 3) manipulation of contract terms so that railroads were forced to enter into long-term agreements and staggering the terms so that no group of railroads would have contracts expiring simultaneously and, hence, would not enter into some individual agreement for some other service agent; and 4) insistence on controlling the type and quality of equipment furnished to the roads.

The government requested that Pullman produce detailed data revealing the sale prices, cost figures, and date of order of every lot of cars sold by the Pullman manufacturing unit to the Pennsylvania Railroad, New York Central, Union Pacific and the Atchison, Topeka, & Santa Fe over a period of several years. Richardson strongly objected to furnishing such data on the grounds that the company was unwilling to reveal the details of purchases by individual railroads because car building rivals might use that information for their own purposes.

Fowler Hamilton, on the other hand, indicated that such data was necessary to prove that Pullman exercised its power to restrain trade in the sale of passenger train cars by reason of different price policies in the sale of "non-competitive" types of equipment, i.e. sleeping and parlor cars, to the Pullman operating unit as compared with the sale of "competitive" equipment, such as coaches, diners, baggage cars, etc., to the railroads themselves. In this manner, the government tried to demonstrate that the manufacturing unit was selling cars to the Pullman Company at prices so high that, by such "subsidy" it could afford to under-bid competitor car builders in selling other equipment to the railroads.

Mr. Hamilton also argued that such data would illustrate whether the directors of certain railroads, who were also directors of Pullman Company, were encouraging discriminatory price policies with respect to different railroads themselves.

Among the first to be called as witnesses by the government were two railroaders, Henry F. McCarthy, passenger traffic manager, Boston & Maine and Maine Central, and Thomas A. Hamilton, traffic manager, Metals Reserve Company, a subsidiary of the Reconstruction Finance Corporation. Both testified that it would not be practical for the railroad to operate their own sleeping and parlor car services and that Pullman was the logical operator. Both witnesses were selected by government counsel in the belief that their railroad backgrounds qualified them to speak as experts on a large number of railroads, and that their testimony would, therefore, constitute evidence for the government's contention that Pullman maintained a monopoly of the sleeping car business for the simple reason that the railroads could not provide their own service and had to, out of necessity, contract for Pullman service.

McCarthy testified, "I don't believe it would be practical for us to do business with any other company that I know of, other than the Pullman Company, to secure cars for our local operations or the cars which we are responsible for in the negotiation of contracts in the through line service. The characteristic traffic flow upon the B&M and MEC varies over a period of years with business conditions and successful salesmanship. The traffic varies considerably, for example, as between summer and winter, holidays and weekends, and normal load days, and demands for equipment also vary depending on outstandingly large meetings, conventions, etc."

In order to demonstrate his point that operation of cars by the railroads themselves would cut their ability to provide cars for peak movements, McCarthy stated that during the winter months his roads operated 22 sleeping car lines in connection with other roads involving 43 cars. On a normal summer weekend, for example, they had 45 car lines with 90 cars operating over their rails. On a Labor Day weekend the road ordered in addition to the latter, about 70 cars from the Pullman pool. These 70 cars originated in their territory and did not include cars ordered by connections. McCarthy added that road-ownership would make interline movements difficult because "nobody would be obliged to furnish the cars in the through line service."

McCarthy offered additional reasons why the operation of sleeping cars by individual lines would be impractical. He indicated that the small scope of operations would not allow as extensive a train personnel to service the cars, and such operation would involve disadvantages from the sales standpoint in that Pullman had a reputation for good service and safety. Finally, he indicated that the purchase of new equipment would involve a huge investment in spare cars which would remain idle a considerable portion of the time.*

When cross-examined, McCarthy testified that the cost of air conditioning on Pullman cars on the B&M and MEC was amortized 75 percent by the roads and 25 percent by Pullman. "If we were to abrogate our agreements with the Pullman Company, we would lose the benefits of future operation of equipment which we have already helped to pay for."

He also testified that even if there were no inherent difficulties in financing sleeping car service, and it could be operated by the railroad as were coaches, the B&M would still have used the unified services of Pullman. When asked why, since the railroad furnished its own coaches for peak periods, it could not likewise furnish its own sleeping cars, McCarthy pointed out that the railroad had accumulated a supply of coaches over the years while it had no sleeping cars in its possession. Also, he indicated, the railroad's spare coach equipment was not up to date, while spare Pullman equipment was, for the most part.

Thomas Hamilton, meanwhile, had been selected because of his railroad career of 42 years and his work in the railroad division of the RFC between 1934 and 1940. He had also been president of the International-Great Northern Railway from 1922 to 1926.

During the course of his testimony, Hamilton stated that, "Catering sleeping car service is a hotel business. It is better done by a specialist—the Pullman Company has set up very excellent standards of service and I doubt if they can be duplicated under individual operation."

He also testified that it was his opinion that it would be feasible for a railroad to own a base lot of sleeping cars and have Pullman own the rest and service both classes, but held that this scheme was not desirable. He pointed to roads which had tried the self-operation of sleeping cars, such as the Milwaukee and Central of Georgia, for example. These roads abandoned the operation, "because it was costing them a great deal of money and they felt that they could afford to be dependent on the Pullman because they would save money."

On another important issue, Hamilton revealed to the court that certain roads were required by Pullman to pay the cost of improvements to a train including the Pullman cars which were included in its consist. The Baltimore & Ohio, seeking to modernize its *Capitol Limited*, was required to pay for modernization of the Pullman cars thereon, even though Pullman would reap the gains from any increase in traffic by reason of that improvement.

Perhaps the most important testimony was that provided by Edward G. Budd, president of the Budd Company. Called as a government witness, he characterized the market for sleeping cars as "hopeless," as far as his company was concerned. Budd, who testified on November 13, was asked whether his company had tried to sell sleeping cars. He replied that, "After the experience with the Santa Fe, we have had a hopeless situation as regarded the market and we haven't paid much attention to trying to sell them. We did have a very vigorous campaign with the Seaboard and we thought we had succeeded in selling them sleepers. Afterwards, we found we didn't get the order."

Fowler Hamilton then examined William K. Etter, vice-president of the Atchison, Topeka & Santa Fe. Fowler's questioning focused on the circumstances surrounding the orders placed by the Santa Fe with the Budd Company for lightweight equipment. Etter testified that an order was placed in 1936 for six 8-car trains of sleeping cars, diners, lounge and baggage-mail cars. He went on to explain

* This is a perennial problem even to this day. Amtrak has sought to address this issue by owning a bare minimum of sleeping cars, an inventory stretched so thin that the corporation has forfeited the ability to meet spikes in demands for sleeping car space during holiday travel periods. For the most part, long-distance overnight train consists are fixed, often unable to match demand.

that the order was subject to change and that the "question of building lightweight equipment was more or less in flux. We hadn't made up our minds what we wanted to do and for the purpose of renting space in the shop where we might be able to get the cars, we placed this definite order for the space in Mr. Budd's shop."

He further testified that the railroad subsequently changed the order as far as the consist was concerned, substituting coach for sleeping car equipment. When asked the reason for this, he explained that rapid changes in car design and a new need for lightweight coaches dictated the move.

Fowler did receive confirmation from Etter that the railroad was negotiating a new contract with Pullman for sleeping car service during this same period, but the witness insisted that there was no intimate connection because the five sleeping cars which the Budd Company did ultimately build for the road, were operated in trains which also contained Pullman-built cars. These Budd-built cars, Etter continued, were operated by Pullman under separate contracts under terms similar to standard contracts with respect to earnings and expenses, but different with respect to amortization.

Ralph Budd of the Burlington testified that operation of its own sleeping cars was not practical for a road on connecting line traffic, yet was feasible for small railroads on local hauls. For example, the Great Northern, which was operating its own sleepers in 1919 when Ralph Budd became its president, later made a contract with Pullman because its own cars were growing old and the growing importance of through traffic and seasonal tourist business made Pullman service more desirable financially and from a service standpoint.

Other witnesses called by the government were W. A. Worthington, vice-president of the Southern Pacific, Daniel Upthegrove, chief operating officer of the St. Louis Southwestern, George W. Hand, assistant to chief executive officer, Chicago & North Western, G. H. Sido, chief operating officer of the Wabash, Edward Flynn, executive vice-president of the Burlington and the Colorado & Southern, and Henry W. Anderson, receiver of the Seaboard Air Line. All of these gentlemen testified that it was more feasible to use Pullman service than to operate their own sleeping cars and that, nevertheless, Pullman service was satisfactory.

Fowler Hamilton also sought to reveal a "community of interest" among Pullman, the New York Central, and the Pennsylvania Railroads by virtue of their interlocking directorates and common banking relations.

Called as a witness was George Whitney, officer of the J. P. Morgan Company, who happened to be a director of Pullman, Inc. and New York Central, as well as a member of NYC's executive committee. There followed a long discussion of negotiations in connection with the absorption of the Standard Steel Company by Pullman, Inc. in 1929 in which Mr. Whitney participated. Here, Hamilton attempted to record the fact that the Mellon Group, which controlled the Standard Steel Car Company, was also interested in the Pennsylvania Railroad. He then directed his examination to the period when the New York Central and Pennsylvania Railroads were considering the purchase of new equipment for the *20th Century Limited* and the *Broadway Limited.* Hamilton asked Whitney whether, "he was worried" at the time that President Frederic Williamson of New York Central

The 1938 editions of both the PRR's *Broadway Limited* and the NYC's *20th Century Limited* were built by Pullman-Standard. Some railroad industry and government officials wanted to know why. *City of Boston* was a 1938 *Century* 17-roomette sleeping car refurbished by P-S in 1946. *PULLMAN-STANDARD, KEVIN J. HOLLAND COLLECTION*

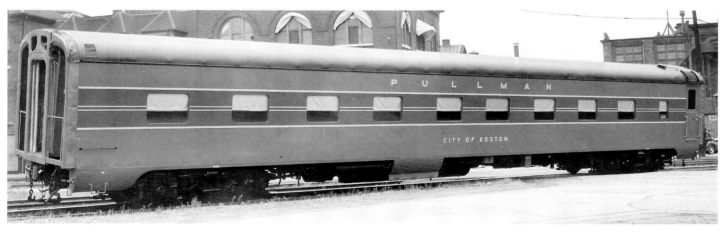

was going to buy cars from the Budd Company.

Whitney replied that he wasn't afraid that Williamson was going to buy the cars from Budd, but rather that he did not understand the situation as between the relative merits of cars built by Budd and those built by Pullman. Whitney declared that it was Williamson's duty as a railroad officer to investigate the possibilities of all types of cars.

Hamilton then introduced documents which allegedly described meetings in the fall of 1938 between officers of the two railroads and Mr. Whitney, during which Mr. Williamson was reported to have questioned the economic justification of large expenditures for lightweight passenger equipment additional to the 52 cars already then purchased from Pullman-Standard. When asked his opinion why the two railroads purchased the new cars at the same time, Mr. Whitney asserted that "the Pennsylvania had already ordered the cars, so the New York Central entered in to keep in the swim."

The final government witness for that day was Henry Sturgess, vice-president, First National Bank of New York and a director of Pullman. Mr. Sturgess answered a key question about Pullman's attitude toward cars built by a competitor by saying that he had it from Pullman management that they would not service sleeping cars made by other companies because to do so would destroy the fundamentals of the Pullman car pool.

After several months hiatus, the trial was resumed on June 1, 1942. Now it was Pullman's turn.

Under questioning by Ralph Shaw, chief of counsel for the defendants, John F. Deasy, vice-president in charge of operations of the Pennsylvania Railroad, stated that unified service in the country's sleeping car business was a natural evolution and it was better for both the railroads and the public. Among the advantages to the individual railroad of a common, independent operation of a large fleet of sleeping cars, he mentioned that the large capital expenditure by the railroad would be eliminated, design and appointments of sleeping cars would be uniform, and a much more thorough and efficient research organization could be maintained for the advancement of the service.

He indicated that the public would eventually have to bear increased transportation charges if individual railroads owned their sleeping car equipment, primarily because the designs of the cars would reflect the ideas of the engineers of the different roads, and the resulting diversity of specifications would result in greatly increased costs as compared with standard designs nationally used. While he believed the Pennsylvania could efficiently operate its own sleeping car services, he added that this procedure would require the railroad to invest in much more expensive equipment that would be idle a large part of the time, whereas Pullman operation afforded the advantage of a large reserve pool available for peak periods. He added further that neither the Pullman Companies nor any of their officers or directors had ever attempted to dictate to, or coerce, the Pennsylvania Railroad as to its operations or equipment purchases.

On June 2, C. A. Liddle, president of Pullman-Standard Manufacturing Company, made the point that there was no written or oral agreement existing between the operating and manufacturing companies that required sleeping cars built for, or operated by, Pullman be constructed by Pullman-Standard, or to prevent that company from building sleeping cars for railroads or any other buyer that might offer to purchase such equipment.

He testified that in the period 1920-1929, Pullman-Standard built 46.23 percent of the passenger cars that had been built in this country. Excluding sleeping cars built for The Pullman Company, the production was 29.47 percent of the total for that period. In the decade beginning in 1930, Pullman-Standard produced 51.18 percent of the passenger cars built in the United States, including sleeping cars built for Pullman operation.

He went on to say that Pullman-Standard was set up for the convenience of the Pullman organization and had always worked closely with the operating company. This was a definite advantage, he continued, particularly in conducting development research, as duplication of effort was eliminated and manufacturing and operating requirements were equally served. He added that progress made by Pullman in the use of aluminum alloys and of low alloy, high tensile steels in passenger car manufacturing was facilitated by this arrangement.

After the testimony of Mr. Liddle, the defense lawyers called E. Eugene Adams, then vice-president of Pullman, Inc. in charge of transportation research. He detailed how plans were formulated for the Union Pacific's first streamlined train, *City of Salina*, and how plans and specifications were submitted to three car builders for bids. At that time, Mr. Adams was a Union Pacific officer and he recommended to Edward Harriman, the railroad's chairman, that the Pullman offer be accepted because of that company's experience in passenger car design and because the aluminum alloy it proposed to use had been tried out in actual railroad service.

David Crawford, president of the Pullman Company and of Pullman, Inc. was called to be the next witness. He testified that the reason for the separation of the operating and manufacturing activities of the Pullman organization was that some Pullman directors were railroad directors and that the Clayton Anti-Trust Law affected relations between Pullman as a car builder and the railroads, to the advantage of their competitors. So the car building business was set up as a separate corporation with different officers and directors to overcome this situation.

He also defended the operation of the sleeping car pool by explaining that the mobility and effectiveness of the reserve car supply was greatly increased by the pool system. Crawford continued that Pullman had experienced very keen competition from the airlines, on one hand and from the railroads themselves on the other, particularly where modern lightweight coaches were in service with substantially lower fares. Between the new railroad coaches and the private automobile, Pullman had lost practically all of its short-haul business, he asserted, pointing out that some 7,000 sleeping and parlor cars normally sufficed to take care of peak business, where 10,000 were required in the late 1920s. He concluded that Pullman, for its own protection, would have had to create a manufacturing division if it did not already have one in order to secure the advantages of concentrated standardized production.

To illustrate his point, he explained how closely operating and manufacturing activities were related by pointing to the expenditure of some $33,000,000 for air conditioning and about $38,000,000 for lightweight modern cars at a time when the operating organization was not earning any money, an undertaking that could not have been accomplished so readily if the resources of the manufacturing division had not been available.

On June 9, the defense called John F. Lane, secretary of the Pullman Company and secretary-treasurer of Pullman, Inc. By means of several graphs and charts, he indicated the course of Pullman's business since its early days.

One such illustration showed that Pullman earnings had varied very closely in proportion to fluctuations in national income between 1900 and 1929, but since that date an increasingly noticeable divergence was creeping in. Pointing to the prospects of greatly increased competition from airlines, automobiles, and the railroad's modern coaches, he feared Pullman's situation would become even less favorable. Already, he commented, Pullman's share of through passenger business had dropped from 48.2 percent in 1929 to 36.9 percent in 1940, and in the east, the drop was even greater, from 46.5 percent to 29.7 percent for the same years.

As if the government felt that it was losing ground, Department of Justice lawyer William L. McGovern reminded the court that the essential charge being pressed against the Pullman Companies was the allegation that Pullman, "as a result of deliberate acquisition by purchase of all their competition, have a 100 percent monopoly of the sleeping car business, and that they have used this monopoly to stifle the development of lightweight trains and that they are using it now to restrict the production of railroad equipment and to impose on the railroads onerous contracts."

David Crawford, in rebuttal, stated that the Pullman Company was not afraid that another sleeping car operating company might be formed to compete with it, since the profits from such operations had been too small to be attractive. There had been ever present, he continued, the possibility that individual railroads might operate their own sleeping cars if it were be to their advantage, and this possibility had compelled Pullman to give the railroad terms consistently more favorable to them as new contracts had been negotiated.

Under questioning by Ralph Shaw, Mr. Crawford explained the circumstances under which many of the prosecution's exhibits were written and outlined the background against which he believed they should properly be considered.

For example, Crawford explained, a statement made by a Pullman officer in a letter between Pullman and a railroad that contracted with Pullman for service, provided that Pullman should have the exclusive right to provide sleeper service. This actually applied, he stated, to a special situation that developed in negotiations with the "granger roads" at the time when lightweight sleeping cars were being introduced. Prospective earnings on these roads did not justify extensive allocations of these new cars—each of which cost two to three times as much as the standard car—so Pullman was unwilling to give the railroads unlimited opportunity to demand them.

These arrangements, he explained, provided that the railroad could draw on the Pullman pool only so long as their regular sleepers were furnished by Pullman, and this was the "exclusive" feature being stressed by the federal Department of Justice.

Only by restrictions of this sort was it possible to protect the integrity of the Pullman pool, Mr. Crawford asserted. If the railroads supplied their own lightweight sleepers and drew on the Pullman pool for other equipment, the earning power of the pool would be lost because they naturally would use their own cars on the high revenue runs, leaving the least profitable for the pool cars. In general, Crawford explained, Pullman's contracts gave the company both the right and the obligation to supply sleeper service on the railroads, and it could not remain in business if it yielded the right and retained the obligation.

Any claim that Pullman would service only the cars it furnished would be contrary to the evidence, he declared, as instances had been cited where the company operated cars manufactured by others.

More to the point, Crawford asserted that Pullman was opposed to "tailor-made" trains because their cars could not be readily replaced when repairs were necessary; the number of cars in a train could not be adjusted to fluctuating demands of service; and construction costs were higher per car than for equivalent cars of a standard pattern produced in large lots. He continued that any departure from "uniform conditions" weakened the effectiveness of the Pullman pool.[20]

Turning to the contention that Pullman required that railroad contracts expire on different dates in order to prevent an opposition service from getting started on a group of roads, Crawford referred to a number of instances where negotiations for new terms were conducted between Pullman and groups representing several lines of similar operating characteristics. While the formal contracts were dated to continue from the expiration of the individual contracts they replaced, they actually were negotiated with a number of roads at the same time, and while such conversations were going on Pullman was continuing service without any contract or any protection against the introduction of a competitor.

He countered government claims by stating that the evidence supported Pullman had steadily introduced modern equipment, and in fact over 450 standard sleepers had been remodeled to include private rooms. All the cars could not be rebuilt at once, of course, so there had been instances where Pullman could not supply such cars to meet every demand, but Pullman had spent about $10 million trying to do it. He went on to counter the government's claim that Pullman had refused to service any sleeping cars built by a competitor. "Any claim that Pullman will service only the cars it furnishes is contrary to the evidence." He went on to say, as an example, that Pullman took part in through-line service with the Canadian roads which provided their own sleeping cars.

Also called to the witness stand was Frank J. Gavin, president of the Great Northern. Gavin explained that the Great Northern had not put a high speed, lightweight, streamlined train in service between St. Paul and the Pacific Coast because it would have been too expensive for the company. In order to reap the full benefit of high-speed passenger equipment, a heavy expenditure for track adjustment would have been required, and maintenance costs would have been increased, with the result that freight operations would have heavier charges to bear. He added that there had been no difficulty about getting lightweight passenger cars for the Great Northern, and in fact, Pullman had tried to persuade the railroad to install some.

Despite the fact that even some of the government's own witnesses stated categorically that the Pullman Company was an ideal agency for operating sleeping cars, on April 20, 1943, the court handed down its opinion holding that "there has been a violation of the Sherman Act," and stating that the "formulation of a decree will await further discussion and hearing upon certain points which may be suggested by both parties." Pullman, Inc., immediately announced that an appeal would be taken.

On May 8, 1944, a decree was entered directing Pullman, Inc. to separate its car-operating and car-building subsidiaries. Freedom of choice as to which should be retained was given, and rather than lose this privilege, the board of directors of Pullman decided not to appeal.

In July 1944, it was decided to retain the car-building company and dispose of the car-operating business. On August 12, 1944, President Crawford announced that negotiations had been opened for the sale of the sleeping car business to the railways and on August 30, 1944, a circular letter was addressed to the railways using Pullman sleeping car service listing the tangible properties proposed for sale at a total price of $81,325,222.

On October 2, 1944, Pullman, Inc., officially notified the court that it had elected to sell its sleeping car business and outlined a plan for disposing of its properties to the railways. Meanwhile, the Pennsylvania Railroad stated that it intended to operate its own sleeping and parlor cars.

Wendell Burge, the new assistant attorney general, filed a "plaintiff's response" to the plan for the separation of the sleeping car business from the manufacturing business, in which he asked the court to reject Pullman's plan for the separation.

The objections that were set forth in the plaintiff's response to the plan came for hearing before the court on March 19, 1945, and on March 22, 1945, the court entered its interim order which provided that Pullman, Inc. could cause the Pullman Company to "offer to treat with the railroads or any other persons for the sale of the sleeping car business and the prop-

erties connected therewith," then owned by the Pullman Company. In addition, Pullman, Inc. could trade with the railroads or with any other persons for the sale of all the shares of stock owned by it in the Pullman Company.

The order also provided that Pullman, Inc. could have one year from the date of the order within which to contract to sell its stock in the Pullman Company or to cause the Pullman Company to contract to sell the sleeping car business and the properties connected with it and to submit to the court the proposed contract or contracts for any such sale.

On May 12, 1945, Pullman, Inc. made a proposal to the railways as a group to purchase the capital stock of the Pullman Company on the same overall basis evaluation that was set forth in the letter of August 30, 1944, for the sale of the tangible properties. What was to follow was the battle for Pullman between the buying group of railroads chaired by Willard Place, vice president finance of New York Central, and Robert R. Young, chairman of the Chesapeake & Ohio Railway and head of Alleghany Corporation, which filed a motion to intervene with the court on August 27, 1945.

Concurrently, railroads over whose lines more than 80 percent of all the railroad sleeping car service in the United States was operated, made an overture to Pullman, Inc. on October 27, 1945, to buy all the capital stock of the Pullman Company. The offer was submitted to D. A. Crawford in a letter from Willard Place, acting as agent on behalf of the group of railroads making the offer. The tender of the offer was made at Chicago by Fred Gurley, president of the Atchison, Topeka & Santa Fe, just one of three railroad executives designated by the group of railroads as a committee to act for them in consummating the purchase of Pullman stock. The other executives on the committee were Gustav Metzman, president of the New York Central, and Ernest Norris, president of the Southern Railway. A little over a year and a half later, on July 1, 1947, the sale would be finalized. The Burlington would join 56 other railroads in joint ownership of the Pullman Company.

In the meantime, this drawing of the lines in the sand would set the stage for the next side-show of the railroads: Robert R. Young vs. New York Central. ◼

6 REFLECTION

The attributes of the articulated train design had demonstrated that in selected corridors of less than 500 miles, a passenger train could operate efficiently and profitably. The Burlington had effectively utilized its *Zephyr* concept, luring passengers off the highways and back to the rails. That concept worked well during the Depression years, a time when highway travel was not as sophisticated and when airline travel was still in its infancy. In the future, the Burlington's fleet of passenger trains would enjoy a greater popularity and use by the traveling public. The Burlington would benefit from the effects of a good reputation for service in the eyes the public, a reputation suffering diminishing

Passengers board the *Pioneer Zephyr* at Quincy, Illinois, in the early 1950s. WALLACE W. ABBEY

The *Flying Yankee* proved to be the sole *Zephyr*-type trainset sold by Budd to a railroad other than the Burlington, and it was a New England institution—under several names in a variety of assignments—for almost a quarter century. *HAROLD K. VOLLRATH COLLECTION*

returns by passenger railroads in the eastern half of the country. The *Zephyr* would be the Burlington's own, a standout from among the others, being closely identified with the railroad, and it would characterize its passenger operations for the next 37 years.

By 1936, much had changed in the country. More highways had been built, more airports were being constructed and airline use was becoming fashionable.

Long-distance travel by train, while generally in a slow decline, was still the preferred manner for many. With the exception of the New Haven, the eastern railroads did not emulate the example being set by the Burlington, relying instead on the tried and true conventional train design and traditions of service. New York Central renovated 1920s-era coaches and produced the *Mercury* trains. They proved to be so popular that the rail-

The Reading Railroad's *Crusader*—with a streamlined observation car on each end—was a five-car bidirectional consist pulled between Philadelphia and Jersey City by a Pacific-type steam locomotive shrouded in Budd stainless steel fluting. *READING COMPANY, KEVIN J. HOLLAND COLLECTION*

road financed additional sets of equipment in order to duplicate the success of the first train. The New Haven had introduced *The Comet*, operating between Boston and Providence, an articulated train designed for speed, but also intended to reduce train operating costs—it was double-ended, thus eliminating the need to be turned at either terminal.

Although the Budd Company had proposed to build a train similar to the *Zephyr* for the New Haven, the railroad chose not to order one from Budd because of its cost. It also chose not to duplicate *The Comet*, but as history seems to repeat itself, some 20 years later it would experiment with the articulated train concept once again, and in the decade of the 1970s, the former New Haven would be the testing ground of another generation of articulated trains.

The Boston & Maine and Maine Central Railroads operated the *Zephyr* look-alike *Flying Yankee* between Boston and Portland, and later elsewhere on the Boston & Maine's extensive northern New England system, but it was the only other railroad to purchase the *Zephyr* by any other name.

The Reading Railroad inaugurated *The Crusader* in 1937, built by the Budd Company, offering coaches, diner, and two observation lounge cars—a train which did not have to be turned at its destination, but which was powered by conventional steam, and later, diesel-electric locomotives.

Still, the *Zephyr* was designed to attract passengers, not necessarily to reduce labor costs, although that was a marginal by-product of the design. By 1936, the railroad had recognized that while articulated trains had their merits in specific cases, not all trains should be articulated. When the *Denver Zephyr* was introduced, the company had decided to follow a course which reverted to conventional individual cars which could be placed into a train, or withdrawn, as fluctuations in service demands necessitated. After 1936, the railroad ceased to order articulated trains, although it did experiment with car design.

This was not the end of articulated trains, however. In the late 1940s and mid-1950s, the articulated concept was revived by Alan Cripe and the creative engineers at Chesapeake & Ohio who,

PREPARING THE WAY OF THE ZEPHYRS

Initiating service of high-speed trains was not something to be done without considerable thought and consideration to the type of track structure that would be required to carry the new trains envisioned by both Ralph and Edward Budd. A track structure which is both safe and uniform in quality is of the utmost importance. In order for the new trains to operate safely, a close examination was made by the Burlington of its existing roadbed before the *Zephyr*s hit the rails.

Track structure is made up of several components which are all interconnected. Every roadbed must be prepared to offer a flat, stable, even surface. This surface is composed of a base which offers good drainage and which is capable of carrying the weight of the heaviest trains that could be expected on that track. For example, a light-density branch line would not be composed of a track structure similar to that of a main line. On top of this surface must be placed a track structure consisting of ties, rails, fasteners, and ballast. Ties are laid on the flat surface to provide a base for the rails. Two "tie plates," contoured plates also known as "fish plates" on which the rail rests, fitted with openings on both sides for the placement of spikes, are laid on top of each tie set to gauge, 4-feet, 8-1/2-inches apart. The rail, whose weight is measured by the yard and which will carry the train (and whose own weight forces the rail downward), is fastened in place on the plates with spikes, which keep the rails from moving laterally so they remain in the proper gauge. This structure is then covered with a suitable ballast composed of a material, such as crushed stone, which keeps the track structure stable.

On the Kansas City–Lincoln run of the *Burlington Zephyr*, the track was laid with 90-pound rail embedded in cinder ballast. The tracks on the Chicago–Minneapolis–St. Paul run were composed of rail weighing 100, 110, and 112 pounds embedded in rock ballast, with the exception of a few places where the roadbed was laid with 90-pound rail on treated ties and gravel ballast. Steam-drawn trains exerted a beating on rails and track structure due to the heavy pounding associated with a steam locomotive's drivers, thus necessitating constant maintenance. The new diesel-drawn locomotives and lighter weight trains made maintenance much easier, and resulted is less daily damage to track, but because of the higher speeds, it was necessary to make several adjustments to track alignments which were not otherwise required by the slower speed of the conventional trains of the period.

In order for the trains to maintain the anticipated average speed of 85 mph, it was necessary for the Burlington to make two line revisions and realign one curve along the Chicago–Minneapolis main line to make the track safe for the new trains. Between Chicago and Aurora, the trains of the Burlington operated over a three and four-track main line. At Aurora, the track diverged northwest as a 107-mile long single-track line to Savanna, Illinois, on the Mississippi River, a line composed of light grades and light track curvature. Between Savanna and St. Paul, a distance of 286 miles, the main line became double-track with maximum grades of 0.2 percent, but with many curves, few of which, however, exceeded one degree.

When the decision was made to initiate high-speed service along this corridor, tests were made using the original *Zephyr* to test the track and determine whether or not a faster schedule

NOVEMBER-DECEMBER, 1941

Burlington Route

TIME TABLES

Way of the Zephyrs

America's Distinctive Trains

To Prevent Waste, Please Keep This Folder

text continued on page 114

could be maintained. The tests were conducted on the existing track structure without modifications. Indeed, when the historic run between Denver and Chicago was conducted on May 26, 1934, track engineers were uncertain exactly what refinements in maintenance to the existing line would have to be made. Fortunately for the railroad, those in the engineering department, and those with experience such as Ralph Budd, were able to determine to some extent what changes, if any, would be necessary for the high-speed run.

In the case of the Chicago–Minneapolis run, on April 6, 1935 using the new *Twin Zephyr* No. 9901, the data gleaned from the previous operation of the *Zephyr* provided the necessary background for track engineers to determine what modifications could be anticipated. So, in preparation for the run, engineers recorded the elevation of every curve on both tracks between Chicago and St. Paul. Any irregularities in elevation were made uniform so that operation at 100 mph could be maintained whenever track conditions permitted. All existing elevations were charted on a condensed alignment map and allowable speed was calculated for every curve, and recorded on the map. Speed restrictions contained in the railroad's operating rules were charted and incorporated as well. What resulted was a series of speed zones being charted for the benefit of the operating department.

From that chart, a schedule was prepared for runs in both directions on both tracks, as the Burlington was an early proponent of moving trains on multiple tracks without regard for the "normal" direction of traffic. The tests were conducted so that they did not interfere with scheduled passenger trains, but not in regard for freight trains, as the dispatchers were allowed to keep them in the clear. Section crews were only given the daily line-up of trains, so preparation work was kept at a minimum to give engineers a reliable test.

Track and mechanical engineers, along with other observers, were placed throughout the train to make note of the riding qualities at various locations along the route. A Sperry track recorder was placed mid-train to check the lateral and vertical movement of the cars and to corroborate the observations made by those riding. System and district engineers rode the cab to keep the locomotive engineer informed of the track and grade alignments and the allowable speeds.

Each observer made notations with regard to the riding qualities of every curve, tangent and turnout so that changes could be made to track conditions, if warranted.

Five-inches deviation was ultimately selected as the maximum elevation. Considering that slower freight trains would also be using the same tracks, special tests were made following the trial run to determine the rate of "run off" from the elevations, or the return to level track. The tests indicated that the easiest approach to a curve was 1-1/4 inches of rise per second at 85 mph, with a run off of one inch in 100 feet. The speed selected for curves was 85 mph as the most suitable, except on restricted curves where the same rate of 1-1/4 inches per second was applied for trains running at slower speeds.

Track engineers determined that there would not be any fundamental changes necessary to the existing construction or maintenance of the track structure, nor was it necessary to make any elevation changes to many of the curves. The reason: the lower center of gravity of the new trains. So, existing elevation was sufficient to produce a comfortable ride even at higher speeds than those of conventional trains. Some curves sharper than one degree, however, did require some elevation, and in a few locations where an elevation in excess of five-inches existed, a speed restriction was imposed.

Engineers faced another issue, that of maintaining train speed for optimum performance. The *Zephyr* demonstrated that the train could accelerate from a standstill to 60 mph in a very short interval, but that above 60 mph, the rate of acceleration dropped progressively. Engineers and operating officials recognized, therefore, that maintaining a sustained speed as much as practicable, within the parameters of safe operation, was most desirable in order for the train to maintain the faster schedule. As a result, only three realignments through switches at junction points were necessary to avoid speed restrictions.

Concurrent with the examination of track structure, the railroad undertook a study to determine if any changes in signaling systems would be necessary. With few exceptions, no changes were needed, although where automatic highway grade crossing signals were in use, modifications were necessary. As each grade crossing circuit had to be set for the fastest train in use on that section of track, approach circuits had to be lengthened in order to accommodate the higher speeds of the new passenger trains.

What the railroad ultimately determined from all these tests was that no fundamental changes in track or maintenance methods was necessary for the safe operation of the Burlington's high-speed *Zephyrs*. In fact, it was determined that even in light of the higher speeds, there would be very little increased maintenance necessary to the track structure. The savings and other advantages brought about by the lighter-weight trains extended across the spectrum of the railroad's safe operation of trains, with ever more emphasis being placed on the comfort and safety of the traveling public.[21]

under the direction of Robert R. Young, were searching for a new train to lure passengers back to the rails and off the highways. These trains, *Aerotrain* (built by General Motors) and *Xplorer* (built by Pullman-Standard) utilized many of the concepts effectively incorporated by the *Zephyr*s and *The Comet*, such as the connections between units as pioneered by Ohio Brass.

The locomotives employed by the articulated *Zephyr*s were unique, custom-made—intended to be a part of the homogenous design of the train. While in the years following the introduction of the first four trains, the locomotives could be separated from the trains they pulled, they looked out of place pulling anything else. In the case of the *General Pershing Zephyr*, its shovel-nosed *Zephyr*-styled engine was the last to be built for the Burlington, or any other railroad for that matter. Yet, lessons learned from these examples paved the way for a new generation of diesel-electric locomotives. Thereafter, standard EMD "E" units, some with stainless steel fluting on their sides, and later the balance of units ordered painted silver, would become the mainstay of the Burlington's passenger locomotive fleet.

By 1941, Budd was filling passenger car orders for America's railroads, big and small. New York Central, having bought a few coaches from Budd before 1940, ordered two train sets for its famed *Empire State Express*, but no sleepers. Other railroads followed.

Although there was war in Europe, the United States had managed to stay "neutral." Even so, war with Germany seemed to be a foregone conclusion. For America's railroads, however, the lean years of the Depression were behind them. For the Burlington, the resurgence of farm and forestry products being transported, along with growing numbers of passengers, boded well for the railroad's future. Plans were being laid for new services which would proudly carry on the reputation established by the revolutionary trains which had so recently heralded a new era in rail transportation. With more business came more revenue and more earnings. The future was bright. Many confidently believed that nothing was going to impede THE WAY OF THE *ZEPHYR*S.

left: *Silver Charger*, built for the *General Pershing Zephyr*, marked the end of the "shovel-nose" locomotive. ELECTRO-MOTIVE, KEVIN J. HOLLAND COLLECTION

below: New York Central turned to the Budd Company for a new edition of the *Empire State Express*, a day train that made its streamlined debut on December 7, 1941. RICHARD J. COOK, ALLEN COUNTY (OHIO) HISTORICAL SOCIETY COLLECTION

overleaf: THE NAVAL HISTORICAL FOUNDATION–PHOTO SERVICE

ENDNOTES

1. "Passenger Service Improvement Sets New Record," *Railway Age*, November 16, 1940, pp. 705-707.

2. "Union Pacific Plans High-Speed Streamlined Train," *Railway Age*, May 27, 1933, pp. 761-762.

3. "Stainless-Steel Train Delivered to Texas & Pacific," *Railway Age*, Nov. 11, 1933, pp.692-694.

4. Overton, Richard, *Perkins/Budd*; pp. 91-93.

5. Ralph Budd, speech before the American Association of Railroad Superintendents, 1935.

6. Overton, Richard, *Burlington Route*; pp. 393-425.

7. Ibid.

8. Harry C. Murphy, speech on the occasion of the presentation of the *Pioneer Zephyr* to the Museum of Science and Industry, May 26, 1960.

9. *Railway Age*, Volume 97, No. 22, December 1, 1934, p. 753.

10. *Railway Age*, April 13, 1935, p. 586.

11. *Railway Age*, October 19, 1935, p. 514.

12. *Railway Age*, November 2,1935, p. 563-565.

13. Ralph Budd, speech before the Cincinnati Business and Professional Men's Group, 1935.

14. *Railway Age*, Volume 100, No. 16, April 18, 1936, pp. 659-661.

15. Aldag, Robert, *Railroad History*, "Diesel Revolution," 2000, pp. 89-94.

16. *Railway Age*, September 19, 1936, p. 426.

17. Letter from Edwin C. Schafer, Dir. Press-Radio-Television Relations UPRR, to R. C. Overton, December 8,1958.

18. Wagner, Hol, "Shovelnoses," *Burlington Historical Society Bulletin* No. 13, Fourth Quarter 1984, pp. 28-29.

19. Ibid.

20. *Railway Age*, June 20, 1942, p. 1172.

21. *Railway Age*, December 15, 1934, pp. 794-796.

BIBLIOGRAPHY

Abbey, Wallace W., "The train that sparked an era," *Trains & Travel* , September 1952.

Baker, George P. & Gayton E. Germane, *Case Problems in Transportation Management.* New York: McGraw-Hill Book Company, Inc., 1957.

Dubin, Arthur D., *Some Classic Trains.* Milwaukee: Kalmbach Publishing Co., 1964.

Overton, Richard C., *Burlington Route.* Lincoln, Nebraska: University of Nebraska Press, 1976.

Overton, Richard C., *Perkins/Budd—Railway Statesmen of the Burlington.* Westport, Connecticut: Greenwood Press, 1982.

Rae, John B., *The Road and the Car in American Life.* Cambridge, Massachusetts: The MIT Press, 1971.

Stover, John F., *The Life and Decline of the American Railroad.* New York: Oxford University Press, 1970.

Swanberg, J. W., *New Haven Power.* Medina, Ohio: Alvin F. Staufer, 1988.

Wagner, F. Hol, "Shovelnoses." *Burlington Route Historical Society Bulletin*, No. 13, 1984.

Wagner, F. Hol, "Aeolus." *Burlington Route Historical Society Bulletin*, No. 14, 1985.

White, Jr., John H., *The American Railroad Passenger Car.* Baltimore, Md.: Johns Hopkins University Press, 1978.

Railway Age, January 1931– December 1964.

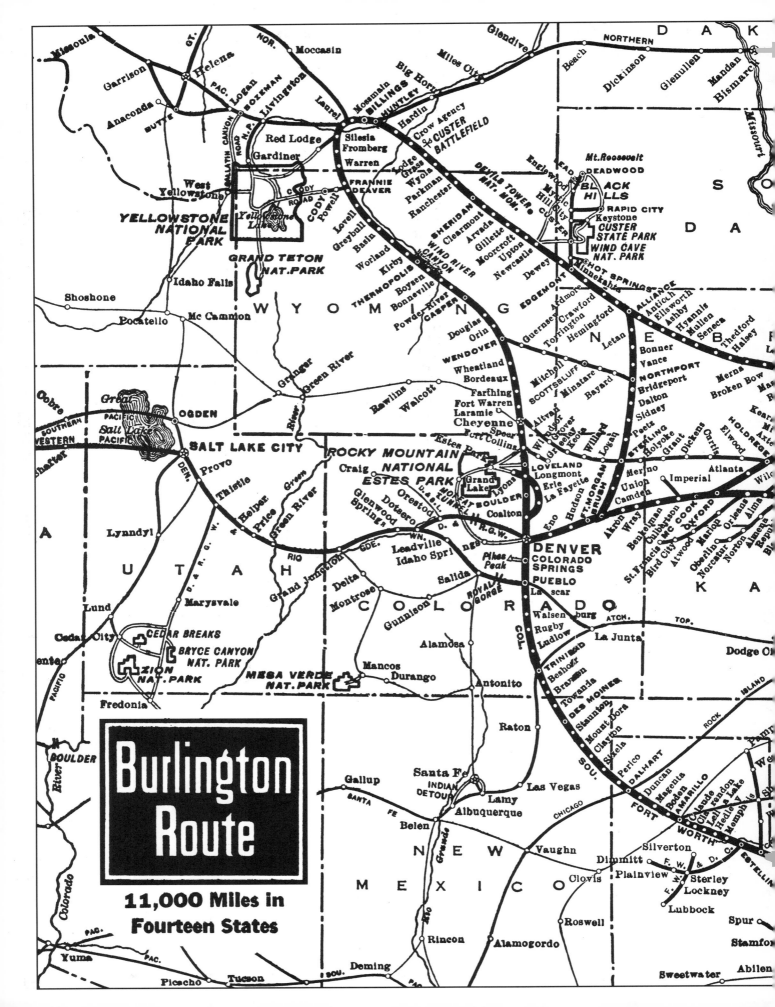

Burlington Route

11,000 Miles in Fourteen States